A Matter of Life and Death

A Matter of Life and Death

Or How to Wean a Man Off Football

RONNI ANCONA

and

ALISTAIR McGOWAN

faber and faber

First published in 2009
by Faber and Faber Limited
Bloomsbury House
74–77 Great Russell Street, London WC1B 3DA

Typeset by Faber and Faber Limited
Printed in the UK by CPI Mackays, Chatham

A CIP record for this book
is available from the British Library

ISBN 978-0-571-25054-7

2 4 6 8 10 9 7 5 3 1

This book is dedicated to Alistair's dad,
the wonderful 'Mac'

WARNING: This book contains wild generalisations!

Football, Football Everywhere . . .

There is a little bird outside my kitchen window looking at me in a strange way. An almost threatening way. I've smiled at him several times but still he sits on the fence giving me the evil eye.

No, he can't be. Obviously he's not. I must be being paranoid. He's probably got far more important things on his mind: like whether the recent absence of next door's cat means he's dead or just has a nasty paw infection, whether he should build an extension to his nest himself or get some magpies in to do it for him, or whether he'll go to my redcurrant bush for lunch or hit the garden hut instead.

One thing I can guarantee he won't be thinking about, however, is football. Or am I jumping to conclusions? You never know. I mean, there is so much football around nowadays that maybe my little bird's tiny brain is full of thoughts about the five-a-side he's set to play in on Saturday against a couple of jays, two blackbirds and a blue tit. Or maybe he's working out whether he's got the energy to fly to Africa to see his favourite team, The Sudanese Spoonbills, play in the Feathered Alliance Cup Final in May. Or maybe he's actually standing motionless on my fence because he's trying to see the latest score of the game blazing away on the television behind me.

What am I doing? I can't believe I'm standing in my kitchen on a wet Wednesday night contemplating whether a little bird would be thinking about football or not. But it just seems that everyone in the world these days *is* thinking about, talking about, watching or playing football. Fundamentalist football fans, I think, will seriously not be content until every man, beast and little bird has been taken over by the doctrine, the religion, the agony that is football. Taken over like my husband – whose attention I have been trying to get for the last ten minutes, but to no avail. Not in a selfish please-gaze-adoringly-at-me-and-say-that-I-look-good-in-my-nice-new-top way but in a patient and generous I've-made-salmon-teriyaki-for-us-and-if-it's-not-eaten-now-it-will-look-and-taste-even-more-unappetising-than-the-burnt-mouse-it-already-resembles way.

But he is catatonic. Why? Because he is watching the football. Yet again! His eyes are glazed over and his mouth is open slightly – almost as if he hopes the ball might drop into it.

I leave the kitchen window, leave my little bird to his strange thoughts, and resort to telling my husband that I am pregnant with triplets. Still not a flicker. With 'the football' droning on in front of him, I am clearly just emitting white noise. There is only one thing for it: either I dance around the room naked, waving the salmon teriyaki in front of him, or I give our dinner to the little bird and just quietly leave my husband to his sainted football. I decide instead to throw the salmon teriyaki on the floor, storm out of the room and slam the door behind me. He doesn't even follow me out to see how I am. There will be words later, inevitably – when 'the football' has finished. An argument of some sort. An argument about 'the football'. And, if you think carefully about the relationships you've had, the relationships you are in, football is probably the cause of more arguments than anything else. You know the sort of thing . . .

HER: *'Why do you have to watch so much football?'*
HIM: 'Why don't you take an interest?'

HER: *'Why is it on television all the time?'*
HIM: 'Why don't you just let me watch it?'

HER: *'All you talked about all night was football . . .'*
HIM: 'If you took an interest you could join in . . .'
HER: *'If you didn't take so much of an interest, you could talk about other things . . .'*
HIM: 'What's so wrong with being a football fan? It's not like I'm a killer . . .'
HER: *'Well, it's killing our relationship – so maybe they're one and the same thing!'*
HIM: 'Be quiet! I'm trying to watch the football.'
HER: *'Murderer!'*

How much better might our relationships become if men treated their wives/girlfriends with the same deference and awe, the same lifelong, blind devotion with which they treat 'The (so-called) Beautiful Game'. 'No chance!' I hear you say.

Because if men are commitment-phobes where relationships are concerned, they certainly seem to apply different rules to their football club, don't they? I mean, think of the popular (and really irritating) football chant 'City/United/Name of Club till I die, I'm City/United/Name of Club till I die, I'm City/United/Name of Club till I die'.

These men are willing to commit themselves to a whole lifetime of association; that football club can do anything to them and they'll put up with it. Their football club is written through them like the name in a stick of rock – until they die. Sad, isn't it?

You see, probably my biggest problem with football – apart from it being constantly on the television – is that it is so overrated. I mean, you can watch a football match for what seems like aeons and when eventually (if eventually) a goal is scored, the display of ecstatic astonishment that follows is just extraordinary!

'It's a goal!' The backslapping! The praise! A goal! Yes, that's what you're supposed to do: score goals, for God's sake! Players are paid thousands of pounds a week to get a ball in a net, and half the time they can't even do that. And if they actually do, then they stop mid-job to congratulate themselves. I mean, what's it comparable to? A surgeon in the middle of an operation, stopping to do a lap of honour around the operating theatre: 'A stitch, I've done a stitch!'

Then there is the endless talking about the wretched game, with friends, with workmates, with total bloody strangers. Was it a penalty? Was he offside? Should he be banned? Will he be fit? Can they still do it? Did they ever do it? Should their goal have been allowed? Personally, I veer on the side that all goals should be allowed, given that there are all too few of them and that goals are the only thing that puncture the monotony.

I suppose when all the football took place on a Saturday, at 3 o'clock, it was just about palatable. There was barely a 'live' game in those heady days, except for the FA Cup Final. And *Match of the Day* only took up one hour, once a week. It had no annoying little cousins with prefixes or suffixes. There was no sneaky *Midweek Match of the Day*. No chummy *Match of the Day 2*. It was easier for the football fan to stay on top of the football world. Easier for non-football fans, like me, to ignore it completely.

But now, the coverage is never-ending. If the football fan

buys into the whole Sky experience (and most of them do), he can watch football, from somewhere around the globe, from some decade or other, at almost *every hour of the day or night*. And that's just the official matches; then there are the 'friendlies'.

So often, as you come back from work, exhausted, looking forward to putting your feet up and idly watching some telly, what do you find in the primetime slot for your delight and delectation? A nice film? A great drama? No! Football!! But is it a big England international? Or an 'all-important' Premier League game? Noooo! It's a 'friendly' – a totally irrelevant game. Officially irrelevant. Not just irrelevant in the way all the other games (as far as I'm concerned) are irrelevant but an *officially* irrelevant game. And yet a game which, because it involves our national team, is still seen as an excuse for even more football coverage!

Perhaps I wouldn't mind the friendlies being televised so much if the sentiment behind the match were as innocent and adorable as its little name suggests. But do we really think Italy's mum phoned up England's mum and asked for 'a play date'?

And the friendly is never friendly on the pitch, is it?

No. Like the whole sport, it is so horribly, continually full of aggression: aggression in the crowd, aggression in the tackles, aggression in the way the players constantly surround the referee and complain about every decision he makes. How many times have I heard myself say, 'But it's only a game! Why are they all getting so carried away?'

And then there's the cheating – which the players don't even have the ingenuity to hide in any way. Even when I cheat at Monopoly, I have the decency to hide my stolen

Mayfair card under the rug. You just don't see the same degree of cheating in other sports. Do you ever see athletes pulling each other's shirts as they come off the bend in the final lap of the 800 metres? No. Do you ever see Roger Federer clutching his eye, pretending that his opponent has hit him with a tennis ball and then falling to the floor to writhe around until his opponent is sent off? No, of course you don't. He wouldn't. Not just because it is dishonourable but because everyone can see that it didn't happen. But that doesn't seem to stop footballers. And footballers are supposed to be role models. Their bad sportsmanship is copied by children and adults alike. They have a responsibility to be, well, responsible.

But the diehard football fan doesn't seem to care what his players do on or off the field. As long as they wear the shirt and kiss the stupid badge, they will support them till they die. Why? Why? I don't understand!

And when I finally convince myself to be patient, when I finally think I can put up with 'the football' being on – just to keep the domestic peace – the sound of it drives me mad. The constant tuneless drone, the primal chanting of the crowd, John Motson's annoying little boy's voice all make me want to scream!

And the noise of football on the radio is just as bad. Oh, the relentless, turgid litany of those results being read out always makes me feel that I am in the midst of some ghastly 1960s kitchen-sink drama – without the drama. My world turns black and white. I can hear whistling kettles, distant babies crying with dirty mouths and mournful trumpet music. For me, it's like having a frontal lobotomy without the anaesthetic.

It also, somehow, rams home to me all the things I'm

never going to get to do in my life . . . like invent something useful or win an Oscar. I bet Audrey Hepburn was never stuck at home with her greying husband arched over a small Roberts radio listening to a man in a box stretching out every syllable in the number of goals scored in a match between Exeter City and Northampton Town as if world peace depended on it.

And I know I'm not alone in all this. So many of my girl-friends feel the same. 'The football' has taken over our lives, our front rooms, our evenings, our weekends, our men . . .

It's time to face up to the fact that football is an addic-tion, a growing addiction – like smoking, cocaine or alco-hol. Some people might say, 'Come on! Football doesn't harm anyone else.' But I believe there is such a phenome-non as 'passive football'. A lot of people around the twenty-a-day football fan get affected by it too. It seeps into our hearts and lungs and minds as well.

If football had a direct, visible-under-an-MRI-scan impact on our health, the government would definitely have looked to ban it by now. It would, at least, carry a health warning: 'Breathing in other people's football can harm you.'

All right, perhaps if I played the game I might under-stand it more. But I've never played football. I know some women do. Some women actually like the game, I know. But kicking a ball, a pointless ball, pointlessly kicking a pointless ball featured for no more than five pointless kick-ing minutes in my young female life.

But sometimes I do find myself wondering: if such a large percentage of the population love it, why can't I get similarly excited about watching a group of men kicking a ball about on a big piece of grass Saturday after Saturday, Sunday after Sunday, week in, week out, month after month, year in, year out, decade after decade? Hmmm, I think I've just answered my own question!

And then, on this wet Wednesday night, as I sit on the stairs with tears in my eyes and salmon teriyaki under my fingernails, I start to imagine how happy millions of women around the country would be if men gave up football. Imagine if I could actually get *my* husband to give up football. Oh, joy! And if I could do it, maybe I could help other women to help their men give up football, and before we know it everything will be better. And I won't be smashing plates of salmon teriyaki or thinking ill of little birds on my garden fence . . .

But I couldn't really do it, could I? Well, why not? I'm an intelligent woman. I bet I could convince my husband of football's ills if I really worked at it systematically! Yes, I'll go back in there and . . . Actually, no. Not my husband. I'm not that stupid. I need a more suitable guinea pig to try my methods out on. I need a friend who it wouldn't matter if I lost in the process . . . but who? Yes! Alistair McGowan! He'd be perfect!

You see, Alistair and I used to go out with each other, lived with each other, in fact, for most of the 1990s. And football was one of the biggest problems in our relationship. At the time, Alistair was doing a lot of football-related work – football-club dinners, football videos, football radio shows, comedy spots on TV sports shows that were mainly about football. He played football three times a week and went to watch football matches every other week. He read about football in the papers, wrote about football in the papers, bought football magazines, watched every football programme going on terrestrial television . . . Football became his life. And slowly started to ruin mine.

ALISTAIR: It didn't ruin it.
RONNI: It did! And anyway, you're not in the book yet, Ali, so be quiet!

I tried to like football when Ali and I went out together. I even went to the FA Cup Final with him once.

ALISTAIR: 1995. Manchester United v. Everton.
RONNI: Get out of my chapter!
ALISTAIR: Sorry!

In fact, I decided there and then to be a football fan. Surely all these excited people couldn't be wrong? I thought. But who should I support? Rather like a floating voter, I kept my options open and waited to see who won the Cup Final before deciding on whom I would forever lavish my affections. Everton won, and I became one of their supporters.

In a new twist, I decided I would support them not 'until I died' but until they lost. It was a short-lived relationship: they lost their next game. I decided I would then support their conquerors until they lost. And so it went on. From Everton to Aston Villa to Chelsea . . . I was involved in some sort of football paper chain but, unlike most football fans, I was always happy – my team was always winning. It was just a different team nearly every week. Maybe I was on to something . . .

But it didn't last.

Alistair's involvement in the sport, however, just grew and grew during our often blissful time as a couple and, as it did so, I began to realise that everywhere I turned there was football.

'What about me?' I used to wonder. 'What's wrong with me? Why are these men in their shiny shorts more important to you?'

So I tried to lure him off the game, to chip away at Alistair's unquestioning love for, acceptance of and devotion to football. At first it was just the odd comment. Little things, like how football didn't make sense (yes, I used the expression 'twenty-two men running around a pitch chasing a tiny ball'), how much time it took up, how totally unattractive Alistair had become as a man, as a human being . . .

And I know it had an impact on him; I know I made at least a dent in his football armour. He admitted as much to me only recently. I got to him sufficiently back then that he is now (ten years later) snorting the game as opposed to mainlining it. Suffice to say, he's still on enough of the hard stuff and yet also susceptible enough for my purposes . . .

He would be the perfect subject for me, for my plan! I grab my mobile and try to lure him around to my house under the pretence that I have Chelsea and England midfielder Frank Lampard in the house.

He knows this probably isn't true, but he is so intrigued that (a) I know who Frank Lampard is, (b) I know that he's a midfielder, and (c) I know that he plays for Chelsea that it is enough to get Ali to come round to see what's going on.

Two hours later, and my master plan is about to get under way – once I've explained to Alistair that Frank Lampard, sadly, had to go (and persuaded my husband to go upstairs and do some work). And made Ali some toast and Marmite.

Alistair has to have toast and Marmite before he does anything. If he'd ever made it as a tennis player, he wouldn't have wanted Robinson's Barley Water or Coke at the change of ends; he'd have had a toaster, a knife and a jar of Marmite on that umpire's chair.

'There's your toast and Marmite.'

'Thanks, Ronni.'

'So what do you think?'

'It's a bit too thinly spread.'

'No! About my idea?'

'You're not serious, are you?'

'Deadly serious.'

'You seriously want men to give up football?'

'Totally!'

'Something that's so close to their heart that it might as well be a . . . pacemaker?'

'Yep. And you're going to be my little guinea pig.'

'I've told you, that all finished when we split up. And anyway, I sold the suit . . .'

'No, Ali, listen. Firstly, I want you to explain to me why men like football so much.'

'How long have you got?'

'And thirdly . . .'

'What happened to "secondly"?' asks Alistair quickly. I'd forgotten how pedantic he can be.

'Secondly,' I add patiently, 'I want *you* to try and give it up.'

'But I don't want to give it up.'

'You do. You just don't know that you do.'

'What is this, *The Ipcress File*?'

'Please, Ali, try and give up football – for me?'

'This a whole life change you're suggesting here.'

'Yes. And you'll thank me for it one day.'

'I can't just give it up.'

'Well, we'll do it bit by bit.'

'No, Ronni!'

'Systematically.'

'You? Systematic?'

'I can be very organised when I want to be, Ali.'

'It's just that you never want to be.'

'Exactly. Or I haven't wanted to be till now. But now I'd do anything to get rid of football. It's taking over the world.'

'But, Ronni, I love football.'

'Do you?'

'Yes!'

'Do you really?'

'Well, I used to love it more than I do now, but I can't give it up. No one can.'

'You only think that because you're addicted, Ali. But all addictions are curable, treatable.'

'You've got to *want* to come off something though.'

'But you *should* want to. It's taken over people's lives. Look how much football there is on television now.'

'There's not that much . . .'

'How can you say that? It's on all the time! And it's all men ever talk about.'

'Listen, I admit there's too much on TV, but it's what makes men, well, men.'

'But you don't want to be one of those men, do you? Just try to give it up, Ali! Think of the things you could do instead with all the time you give to silly football!'

'Steady on! Look, if you really want to wean anyone off football – and I'm not saying I'm in any way committed to this yet – the first thing you have to do is stroke the cat before you hit it.'

'What cat?' I say.

'Oh, it's a management technique for getting someone to change something about themselves. In offices, they say, "You have to stroke the cat before you hit it."'

'Are there that many offices with cats in them?'

'It's just a metaphor.'

'It's a nice idea, though: you could stroke them at moments of stress. Although I'm not sure about hitting them. I don't think you should hit cats.'

'Right . . .'

'What have cats got to do with football again?'

Ali is staring at me blankly.

'I'm just saying, Ronni, if you want to tell someone something negative about themselves – like they've wasted their entire lives by watching football – you have to make them feel good about themselves first. Got any more toast?'

'Yes. But that's the end of the Marmite,' I say with a shrug.

'How can you *run out* of Marmite? Always, *always* keep a second jar!'

Now my job was going to be even harder. I buttered him up by offering him some Twiglets in a sandwich – that seemed to do the trick. I set to it again. I wasn't going to give up. And there was a look in Ali's eye that I recognised. It meant that he'd seen some sort of a personal challenge. And Ali loves a challenge.

'So, Ali,' I say, beginning to metaphorically stroke, 'tell me, what good things has football done for you?'

'Well, it taught me maths. And geography.'

'Football did?'

'Seriously. I only know anything about the geography of Scotland because of football. Hearing the results on a Saturday, as a seven-year-old, and updating my *Shoot!* League Ladders.'

'Your what whattie whatters?'

'They were . . . oh, it's too complicated. And emotional. Anyway, I'm just saying I was made aware of places like Montrose and Arbroath, Stenhousemuir and Ayr by football. And I still dream of going to those distant Scottish towns one day and seeing what those strange names represented all those years ago. What majesty! What beauty! What romance!'

'I come from Scotland. Prepare to be disappointed.'

'Really?'

'No. I'm joking. They're very nice places; well, three of them are.'

'I'm just saying, Ronni, that you can learn from football. About other things than football.'

'So what else did you learn? Where Shakespeare got the inspiration for his stories? How to split the atom?'

'My basic mental arithmetic is very good.'

'Thanks to football?'

'Yep – working out how many wins and points Leeds needed to win the title or escape relegation. It's a great aide-memoire too.'

'A whattie?'

'It helps you remember things. My friend Dan's house number is 62. How do I remember that? Jimmy Greaves. It was the year he played for England in the World Cup Finals in Chile. 62.'

'You could just think of it as the number after 61 . . .'

'The year Tottenham did the double, of course.'

'Of course.'

This was not going to be easy.

'Football, Ronni, football has taught me and millions of men like me geography and maths. It's nourished my competitive spirit, given me thrills, made me shed tears . . .'

'Oh, pur-leaze!'

'By the time you're seven it's in your blood.'

'"Till you die"?' I ask, sarcastically.

'Maybe. If you asked the average man in the street, he would probably say that football has been the longest relationship, the best girlfriend, he's ever had.'

'A-hem,' I cough indignantly.

'Bar one, obviously, in my case.'

'Thank you, Ali. I am clearly better than football.'

'I was thinking of someone else,' says Alistair. 'And, like a girlfriend, football has taught a man how to weather disappointment. Like a girlfriend she's taught him to be patient. Like a girlfriend she's drained him of large amounts of time and emotional energy, and you have to respect that, don't you?'

'Okay,' I admit, grudgingly. 'So if I acknowledge that football's done some amazing things for you and then remind you how it's also made you dangerously obsessive and worryingly dull, will you give it up?'

'For good?!'

'Well . . . let's say . . . for a year?'

There is a long pause. A very long pause. A lot of frowning and lip-chewing.

'I'll think about it,' says my oldest friend.

Ali always says he'll think about it. He thinks he's being enigmatic. He's not being enigmatic. He's being annoyingly stubborn and typically non-committal. As he thinks about it, I'm convinced more than ever that I have to persuade him to give up football and everything to do with it – even if it is in his blood. In fact, particularly because it's in his blood.

Basically, he needs a transfusion – although he'll be transfused with a different blood group, obviously. A blood group without football in it. So, actually, it isn't like a real blood transfusion at all – where you have to be transfused with the same blood group or you die. Anyway, I have to get football out of his blood somehow.

He finally stops chewing his lip and looks at me doubt-fully.

'More Twiglets?'

2

In My Blood . . .

So, Ronni wants me to give up football!

I went round to see her last night; she was raving about Frank Lampard being in the house. I thought she was either becoming unhinged or being burgled by a slightly overweight sporting celebrity and went to help her out.

Then she conveniently sprang this idea on me. Waking up this morning, I thought it had been a dream. It was like I was going out with her again. And we were living in Clapham again. And eating overcooked spaghetti and underflavoured bolognaise again (Ronni's speciality) and she was badgering me about the evils of football.

Even then, Ronni had tried to point out the negative side of football to me, to show me how much of my time it was taking up. But there was no way I could have totally given up then or now.

Or could I?

I love football. Most days begin with me reading the back pages of the newspaper and most days end with a quick look at the results on Ceefax. Sound familiar?

For most men, football is a life choice. Once you're in, you're trapped. It's like a personal pension scheme. You put all this effort and money and time into it and don't get back anything like what you had imagined 'at the end of the day'. You know that but you can't give it up. It's like cigarettes and alcohol: it makes no sense really, I suppose, but you do it because at some point someone, somewhere got you addicted.

I guarantee any man who hasn't fallen in love with football as a small boy is now either a dancer in a West End show or a mini-cab driver who only works until four in the afternoon and then goes home to play backgammon on the internet. Or he likes rugby.

I mean, she's right: there is too much football on television. It is overrated. It does stop men from talking and thinking about the wider issues of the world. It is a refuge. But my love affair goes back to when I was four. It's part of me, part of what makes me a man. It balances my love of neatness and musicals. Could I seriously tidy up and listen to *Hello, Dolly!* as often as I do without also having a healthy dose of football in my life? No. To give it up would be impossible. Emasculating. I *won't* do it!

Seeking to re-establish my maleness – and because there were a couple of games played last night in the lower leagues – I switch on the television and press the text button on the remote.

Page 302 – the football headlines with my morning toast and Marmite. Then the league tables on pages 324–7. Pages beloved of every football fan in Britain. There is probably an easier way to access all this info in this technological age – you can probably have it sent to your brain via your mobile or something – but Ceefax is what I've done for twenty years and the habit, the comfort, the tradition of it is part of my life.

I read and scour the neat lists of place names and numbers, division after division. Half an hour has gone by when I find myself still staring at League Two (the old Fourth Division) and working out how many points

Rochdale are from the play-off places, when I wonder why I'm doing this.

There is a whole world outside. There are birds and clouds; hills and trees. There are films and books and plays and music to be seen and read and seen and heard. What does it matter to me – a man who has never been to Rochdale, a man who could barely point Rochdale out on a map of England (or a map of Rochdale). I know that their ground is called Spotland and that they haven't been outside the bottom division of English football in over thirty-five years, yes. But why, right now, do I need to know in what position Rochdale lie in the football league tables, with how many points and what goal difference? Why does it matter? There isn't going to be a test. And yet I've done this in some form or other since 1971. It's tradition, it's habit. It's addiction.

And I thought I had this under control.

I call Ronni.

'You're right, Ronni. I've got a problem.'

'And you're going to let me help you?'

'I don't know about giving it up but I'd like to cut down.'

'Okay . . . well, that's a start.'

'I just found myself looking at Ceefax and working out how many points Rochdale were off the play-off positions and I . . .'

'Hold your horses!' Ronni has a fondness for outdated expressions. 'Firstly, does anyone still use Ceefax? Thirdly . . .'

'What happened to secondly?'

'Secondly, what are play-off positions? And thirdly, who are Rochdale?'

'Exactly!'

'Okay, this is the first thing you've got to do for me. Are you listening . . .?'

Ronni has a mildly annoying habit of asking you if you're listening to her when you clearly are. She is either buying herself time while she thinks what she's going to say, or she knows that if she were the one listening, her mind would be wandering all over the place and would need calling back to attention.

'You must', she says, 'work out where your addiction comes from, why it started. And then, maybe, we can look at why you still need to feed it.'

'This sounds like analysis.'

'It is. In a way. It's also what happens in Hitchcock's *Spellcheck*.'

'What?'

Ronni has a problem with proper nouns – she always calls things what she wants them to be called, not what they are called.

'It's *Spellbound*, not *Spellcheck*.'

'That's what I said.'

And she doesn't ever believe she does it.

'Anyway, Ingrid Bergman says it to Gregory Peck. We need to find the root cause of your problem and then, if we can acknowledge that connection, cut that link with the past, maybe we can make you better.'

'That was a terrible Ingrid Bergman impression.'

'I wasn't doing her, I was just vaguely quoting the sentiment of the film.'

'Okay. Shall I come round?'

'No, come tomorrow. But promise me you'll think about this, Ali.'

Ronni, like an earnest six-year-old, always wants everything promised. It was only at the age of twenty-eight that she stopped following it up with 'cross your heart and hope to die'.

'I promise,' I say.

'Cross your heart and hope to die?' She's obviously recently lapsed back into that old habit.

'Yes.'

'Yes, what?'

'Cross my heart and hope to die,' I mumble.

'Well done, Ali! You're doing this for the nation. For the men of the country and for the women of the country. Imagine pleasing thousands of women at the same time!'

'I often do . . .'

'Stop it!'

I put the phone down. I had a problem. And I'd acknowledged it. I felt like an alcoholic at his first AA meeting. I'd stood up and I'd said it: 'I'm Alistair and I have a problem with football.' I looked in the mirror. I felt like the smoker who's just realised that everything they own, everything they touch smells of old smoke, that the warnings on the packets aren't just there to teach people the words for 'Smoking Kills' in ten different languages. I felt like the sinner in those films where everyone's wearing dungarees and dusty hats who's just run into the church and shouted, 'Brothers and sisters, I have seen the light!'

Everything was clear. I was an addict and I needed help. Now, what had she said? My 'root cause' . . .?

My father played football with me in the garden from a young age. A ball is one of the first things a father will buy for his son. Even before the child can walk, chances are that the impatient dad will hold his gurgling boy behind a ball and encourage him to swing a puppy-fat leg at it. My dad was a fine footballer, cursed with bad eyesight. In fact, he was a fine all-round sportsman. He grew up in Calcutta as an Anglo-Indian (as I discovered three years after his death on BBC One's *Who Do You Think You Are?*) and had been chosen for India's hockey squad for the 1948 London Olympics, but chose not to go for reasons which even the BBC's researchers couldn't uncover. He'd been asked to go to America to train as a professional boxer but again had not followed up the interest. He played every racquet sport available (frequently barefoot) with a natural instinct, a smile on his face and a pipe in his mouth.

And, after moving to Worcestershire and marrying my mother, he'd played football for the local team in Offenham well into his forties. When I was a boy, he'd regale me with stories of spectacular goals he'd scored, and in my mind My dad was a mixture of Bobby Charlton (the hair), Pelé (the build and the eyes) and Stanley Matthews (the wizardry and the age). When you believe that your father is three of the greatest footballers ever to have played the game rolled into one, you're going to be hooked.

My father was a schoolteacher, so our hours were the same and we played together in every free moment: tennis, badminton, squash, chess, draughts – and football. We wore patches in the lawn in every garden of every house we lived in. I was normally in goal, throwing myself around, and Dad would take shots at me. High, low, soft, hard, left foot, right foot, on the volley . . . 'Catch it!' he'd shout, as annoyed as Brian Clough if I spilled a shot or palmed one away into the chrysanthemums for 'a corner'.

Strangely, my father had never really followed the professional game to any degree before I came along. Not being born in England, he had no connection with any city or club, and our home in Evesham was a long way from any professional ground.

But, in 1970, we went on holiday to Barmouth in North Wales (everybody went on holiday to Wales then) and stayed at a B & B called Hydrangea House. One of the other guests at this tiny little place was a seventy-year-old woman called Mrs Drury, from Leeds. She and I adored each other from the off and, at the end of our week, I was sad to leave the sand, the waves, the strange breakfast of mini-cereals and half-grapefruits but, more than anything else, I was sad to leave Mrs Drury from Leeds. But from then on I was a Leeds United fan and, as Leeds United happened to be the best team in the world at that time, I was forever to thank my lucky stars that Mrs Drury hadn't been born twelve miles down the road in Bradford.

It was a quixotic choice of club. Leeds was 250 miles from Evesham and, as my father drove more than six miles only once a year on our annual holiday to Wales, trips to see them play were clearly going to be somewhat limited.

The first football match I actually went to was two years later at West Bromwich: West Bromwich Albion v. Leeds United. The Mighty Leeds. My Leeds. It was towards the end of the 1971–72 season, and Leeds needed to win the match to stay top of the First Division. There must have been 40,000 people there that day. We found a spot right at the back of a huge bank of terracing along the side of the pitch. There was only one problem: I couldn't see anything.

Gamely, my father picked me up and placed me on his strong shoulders. And there I sat – for ninety minutes. To his last days, he would still talk about the time he very nearly lost all feeling in his neck in order to let me follow the fortunes of my eleven heroes in the white shirts, shorts and 'stockings'. Perhaps he knew that my biggest hero was holding me on his sweating back.

I think my dad might have thought that by going once into this noisy, smoky man's world and by driving into the decaying heart of the Black Country, I might be put off going to live games. But he was wrong. I loved it!

And so it began. Soon we were heading off around the Midlands (most of the teams in the area were in the First Division in those days) to watch Leeds United.

I had pictures of the Leeds players all over my bedroom wall, covering my school books, in front of my eyes when I closed them at night. They were from another world. Men. Supermen. Gods. I still have a book of their signatures – Leeds United players in an official Leeds United autograph book. Peter Lorimer, Eddie Gray, Norman Hunter, Paul Madeley, Terry Yorath, Allan Clarke . . . Names that would mean nothing to youngsters now, nothing to most women of my own age, but to me, then, they were precious, prized and priceless.

So that was my 'root cause'. My father. And Mrs Drury. Back gardens in the Vale of Evesham and Hydrangea House in Barmouth. And it's led me to looking at league tables on Ceefax first thing in the morning, aged forty-three (when I could be doing a hundred other things), and working out Rochdale's chances of making the play-offs.

I had to tell 'Ingrid Bergman' . . .

3

Self-Help Help

Step One: Find the Root Cause

I couldn't believe Ali had said 'Yes' to the plan! Or that I thought of his first step so quickly! Well, actually I can believe both things for two reasons: (1) I've always been a very good improviser, and (3) I've always been able to make him do what I want him to do in the end. Not that he's a pushover. Ali can be incredibly stubborn and never forgets – like an elephant. He can bear a grudge too – like a . . . bear. And he's incredibly competitive – like . . . an elephant-y bear. Competitive. In everything. So it is not going to be easy.

But he'd said 'Yes'!

Then I suddenly realised that although I had achieved my first ambition, I now didn't actually have a plan. No plan at all. Nothing. Nada. Zip.

I needed a programme. I couldn't just say 'Stop it', tap Ali's nose and hope he wouldn't have anything to do with football ever again. No. I needed to work out a proper 'Twenty-Step Programme' to help Ali give up his addiction. But I had to work fast before he changed his mind. He's always changing his mind about everything. I think it's because he's a typical Sagittarius: half man, half beast. Fortunately, he draws the line at always carrying a bow and arrow, and sadly he doesn't have a tail.

Maybe, I thought, I should see what other self-help

books were like, how they sort out and lay out their twenty-step programmes. Yes, I clearly needed to do some research. I don't know as much about self-help books as you might expect – considering how much in my life I need to help myself with. I haven't really read any. Well, I've started them but never seem to be able to finish them. Really what I need is a self-help book to help me finish self-help books.

I go to my friendly local bookshop and start thumbing through *12 Ways to a Happier You*. The passing assistant nods her head and smiles in a sympathetic 'about time too' way.

'Oh, no, it's not for me!' I bleat, defensively.

As I leaf through five or six more of these well-thought-out, simply titled and clearly numbered programmes, full of well-presented psychological and sociological research, positivity and **bold type,** suddenly I feel worried about the task I've set myself. What are my steps going to be? Am I out of my depth here? I can talk a good anti-football game but can I put it into action? It means being ordered and making lists. I'm hopeless at all that stuff. For a start, my brain's a total mess.

The inside of my head generally looks like Clapham Junction. How I long for a fabulously ordered brain! Something like Kelly Hoppen's walk-in wardrobe would do me. You know, lots of little drawers full of crisply laundered thoughts, shelves of neatly ordered intentions and rail upon rail of witty sayings (colour-coded), with the few messy indecisions in one corner waiting to be sorted through instead of being strewn everywhere waiting for my sparking neurons to trip over them.

Perhaps when I'd got Ali off football, I'd read all these

books properly – from cover to cover, one after the other – and get my head in order. And then put them neatly on shelves. Above a special laminated label. Yes, I would. I'd do all that. But then maybe I wouldn't be me any more. I actually quite like my disorder; Ali always used to say it was 'charming – to a point'. And then, I suppose, he reached that point. And that was the end of our relationship. I hated his football dependency; he hated my messy head . . .

By the time I take my armful of books to the till, the manager has come out from the little back room where they always seem to be making horrible coffee and joined the sheepish-looking assistant at the counter. They look at each other furtively. I wonder if I have something on my face: a bit of breakfast, perhaps, or a child's plastic toy. And then I quickly remember the armful of self-help books that I'm cradling to my chest.

'Are you okay, Ronni?' asks the manager, touching my arm. 'Susan was a little concerned . . .'

'Oh, those! These! Yes. They're not for me.'

'We know the signs, Ronni,' she said, nodding slowly while simultaneously seeming to try and swallow her own lips.

'But seriously. I'm trying to seek inspiration from them . . .'

'Yes . . .?'

'For a twenty-step programme of my own. To try and . . . get someone off . . . something . . .'

'Is it drugs?'

'No. Football.'

'Football?'

'Yes. I've a friend who's . . . an addict, I suppose. And I thought I could help him. And maybe, in time, help other football addicts.'

'Addicts? Interesting. I never thought of football as an addiction.'

'But it is, isn't it?'

'Oh, yes! My Pete can't stop reading about it and watching it and talking about it. It's all I hear at home. That awful John Motson's voice whining on. Not to mention that bloody Scottish one on Sky! Two things though, Ronni.'

'Yes?'

'It's always a twelve-step programme.'

'Oh, thank you. That makes it easier then. And what was the third thing?'

'You mean the second thing?'

'Yes. The second thing.'

'You've got a little plastic dog stuck to your cheek.'

As I leave the shop with my arms full of inspirational texts, I wonder what my twelve steps will be.

I walk past the Open Air Theatre in Holland Park. That's it! Maybe I could take inspiration from the ancient Greeks! There's this fabulous Greek play called *Lysistrata*, in which the women of Thebes withhold all sexual favours from their men until they stop fighting with the men of Sparta. And all the women of Sparta join them to stop the warring. This results in all the men wandering around in priapic states, normally with huge strap-on phalluses, which does wonders for inter-cast relations and also leads to the war being called off. It's definitely something that should be tried now in any number of world conflicts. If the women of the world got together – and God knows we could do it nowadays through the wonder of the internet – and all withheld any sexual activity until men adhered to our wishes for peace, the world could be a much happier place.

It is, however, probably not step one in my battle to get a man off football. It would, after all, only be a short-term cure. Besides, the sight of millions of football fans wandering the streets in their polyester England shorts with stonking erections is too horrific to contemplate. Somehow, a few angelic ancient Greeks with curly hair, tunics and stiffies is easier to cope with as an image.

As I get home and put my self-help books in a hopeful, neat pile on the messy kitchen table, I notice my husband has left the computer on. He's been looking at his football club's website again. One great thing about Alistair is that he is not into the online side of football. That needn't be a step at all. But every club has its website now, and men spend hours on them. There are also endless computer games to be played, games for small boys, big boys and grown-up men-boys – my friend Jenny's husband often plays something called Championship Manager well into the night.

Alistair, however, has only just updated his house phone from Bakelite to plastic, still thinks 'Googling' is something to do with the Boy Scouts, that Facebook is a music magazine, that YouTube is a Scottish insult, and he has his own personal definition of a joystick. Unbeknown to him, you can now get instant internet access on mobile phones and BlackBerrys; you can find out the scores and even see the goals from countless games as they happen and watch them again and again and again. The mobile phone has ruined any last chance of football-free zones. There is no haven. No 'getting away from it all'. No mystery. No peace. Not even abroad.

The most horrid thing about the addict fan being able to read results on a mobile is the 'anytime, anywhere' aspect of it. A lovely stroll in the country totally loses its charm when your partner is forever stumbling over tree roots as he stares at his mobile screen. Why can't they just wait till they get home to peruse their silly league tables and results? They'll say that they need to know the latest scores and results as they come in. Why? What are they going to do? Get in the car and drive to Leicester or Huddersfield or the home town of whichever sorry little team they support to buy all the players a congratulatory drink? Or give them a bollocking if they've lost? No, I don't think so. Either way, you can't win. If you're out and about and he sees his team has lost, chances are he will be plunged into gloom and the rest of the outing will be a washout. If they've won, he will still be lost in thought, silently working out what this now means for their chances of reaching the play-offs or of qualifying for the Champions League or God knows what else.

There is a constant connection to the game. If Ali was a technophile, I wouldn't even have got him round to my house. He would have known where Frank Lampard was; it's probably possible to follow him on the Chelsea website's player-cam or something equally pathetic.

I look at my pile of books, full of hope and the promise of a better life. The promise of change. I am hopeful just looking at them. I pick up a book about alcoholism and start to flick through it.

Hey, maybe one of my first steps should be like the bit in the Alcoholics Anonymous programme when alcoholics are encouraged to go and apologise to everyone who has been affected by their addiction. Yes! No. To ask Ali to apologise to everyone whose life he'd blighted by his passion for football – especially the wives and girlfriends of all the people who had bought his football videos over the years – would take for ever. He wouldn't agree to that – even if it did mean lots of nice train journeys.

There is so much to read, and no time to read it. I need to sort my programme out and I have to act fast.

I put the television on. I need a breather. I'll work out my plan in a minute. A trailer comes on for *Match of the Day*. Oh, that music! I hate that music! It's the sound of division. The first division between man and wife. Pleasure for him; hell for her. And do they really need to trail it? Surely it has its audience, *Match of the Day*. And then it hits me. Yes! That great beast will be my first target! I'll write it down straightaway. My list is under way! My programme! Or it will be when I can find a bit of paper . . .

4

Why Women and Football Don't Go

I'm in a taxi on my way home from *Cabaret* (I'm currently playing the part of the 'Emcee' in the West End production and loving it). Ronni's plan is going through my head. I know I've said I'll do it; this morning it all seemed so clear. But now, returning home, with the driver listening to TalkSport and the endless, wonderfully inane chatter about football, I can't be so sure. I try not to listen but my inherent interest in all things football gets the better of me. 'Is Arsène Wenger losing control at Arsenal?' seems to be the theme of the calls.

'Opinions', as my friend Jonny Maitland always tells me, 'are like arseholes; everybody's got one.' And, where football's concerned, everyone's got bagfuls.

I am on the point of asking the driver if *he* could give up football for a year, when he swears at a caller. He swears quite violently. I carry on looking out at the darkling beauty of late-night London going past the window.

One of the best 'football and women' stories I've ever been told was told to me by a London cabbie. He was, he told me, 'like me dad before me' a Spurs fan – 'for me sins'. (This is, by the way, an expression I hate. What sins are these? Murder? Lechery? Stealing? Coveting a neighbour's ox? And at what point were these 'sins' transmuted into following Spurs?) Anyway, 'for his sins', this driver supported Spurs. In fact, he was a season-ticket holder, i.e.

someone who has bought, in advance of the new football season (which will run from August to May), a book of tickets (or frequently nowadays, a credit card-type affair) which entitles the holder to a seat for every game their team will play at their home ground that season.

'So,' he tells me, 'first game of the season, lovely hot day in August, there's these two empty seats in front of me and me mate, right? And I looks at the seats and I says to me mate, "That's typical, innit? All these corporate people nowadays, buying up these seats and then not turning up. 'S criminal! There's two real fans who've not been able to see this game today." 's not right, is it?'

'No, it's that sort of . . .'

'And this 'appens again next 'ome game, right?'

'Right.'

'Same two empty seats in front of us. And the next game. And the next. Everyone's clocked it by now, right?'

'Right.'

'And eventually I says to me mate, "When these people show up, we've gotta give 'em a 'ard time. Wasting these seats." And the club don't care 'cos they're getting the money anyway, right? But it's the principle, innit?

'So this goes on for three months, right. Every 'ome game, full 'ouse – two empty seats in front of me and me mate. And friends of mine wanting to go to see the Spurs who can't get in. So we says again, me and me mate, "When these fu**ers show up, right, we got to give them a 'ard time." People like them are spoiling the game for the true fan. So it comes to Boxing Day, right? And finally this geezer turns up with 'is kid, right? And I think, "Well, 'e's got 'is lad with 'im, so you got to take it easy, 'en't ya?" But I leans forward, before the game starts, right, and I says to this geezer, "Sorry, mate, but I've got to say, these seats 'ave been empty for the last ten games and now you've finally, actually turned up from Spain or wherever it is you live and thought you might as well see a game. I mean, what's goin' on? If you don't want the seats, give the tickets to us, 'cos we've got a lot of friends who'd love to see a game at The Lane."

'Anyway, the geezer turns to me, right, and he says, "It's not my fault," he says. "My wife," he says, looking all sheepish and that, "my wife bought me and my boy the season tickets in August – as a Christmas present! She only gave them to me yesterday."

'Brilliant, eh? She bought 'em for 'im and didn't give 'em to 'im till Christmas! She thought the season went from year end to year end. Poor geezer! Half the ticket wasted!'

'That's brilliant!'

'But that's women and football for you, innit? They 'aven't got a clue.'

'You're so right!'

Without football, what would I talk about to these men's necks and backs . . .?

5

An Immovable Object

Just as I found myself sipping my morning coffee, patting myself on the back for having started to work out my twelve-point programme and wondering whether Alistair had found the root cause of his football addiction or whether he'd been too busy reading the results on Ceefax, there was a dull buzz on the entryphone.

It was Ali, looking frazzled and breathless, as if he'd run the two miles from his place to mine. Or at least walked it really quickly because he was late. He's always late. He says he caught that off me too.

Perhaps I don't have persuasive powers. Perhaps, by a strange osmosis, he's just ever so slowly turning into me, like a weird version of Benjamin Button, and, by the age of eighty, we'll be indistinguishable.

'This is never going to work, Ronni,' he says, breathlessly. 'It goes too deep.'

'You look frazzled.'

'I just ran here. I'm late!'

'Oh, that's not like you.'

'But I've been thinking about my "root cause", my first taste of football, where it all . . . And look, maybe I could just cut down a bit. Maybe not check the League Two scores quite so regularly or something. But I'm sorry, I can't give it up completely. I just can't!'

'Yes. Yes, you can.'

'No, a man's relationship with football . . .'

'Is this going to get deep?'

'Yes . . .'

'Then you'd better come in.'

It was early in the morning but Alistair was already happy to talk philosophy. I've never known anyone get out of bed with his head so switched on. He would put it down to not drinking: he always has a clear head. He doesn't even need coffee in the mornings to get him going, for God's sake!

While I was thinking all this, he was still talking. I don't think I'd missed anything . . .

'So a man's relationship with football, with his football club is forged in the family unit. And the bond – especially between a father and a son – though often in later life a painfully silent one – generally has football at the heart of it. It's the one thing you can always talk to your father about – football. As time goes on, most other things you tell your mum, and she just sort of passes them on to your dad, over some soup. But football is what unites a father and a son. And you see, Ronni, by remaining loyal to football – to his football club – the adult male has a constant part of his father within and around him, comforting him, reminding him. That's why he can't let it go . . .'

'He or you?'

'He and me. Him and I. All four of us.'

'So you got your love of Leeds from your dad?'

'No, but my love of the game is all bound up with my dad. That's why I can't give it up.'

'Ummm . . .'

Ali was going to be a harder nut to crack than I thought; I know how much his dad ('Mac') had meant to him.

'But for most men, you're saying, it's likely that their team was their father's team?'

'Yes, Ronni. And their father's father's team.'

'Yes.'

'And their father's father's father's team.'

'Right.'

'And their father's father's father's father's team . . .'

'All right!'

'. . . which probably takes us back to about 1888.'

Alistair paused, as if his point was totally proven. If he'd been to a good school where they'd had a tradition in Latin, he would certainly have said 'QED' at this point.

'What's so significant about 1888?'

'That's when the Football League started. The FA Cup was 1872 and the actual game had been around in some form since medieval times but . . .'

'How do you know all that?'

'It was in the *Ladybird Book of Football*.'

'Oh, God! Anyway, 1888, you say, was when this whole sorry business started to afflict women around the world, right?'

'1888. The start of the Football League. Yes,' said Alistair, starting to sound like Dustin Hoffman in *Rain Man*, whose autism I was, worryingly, starting to compare with my oldest friend's condition.

'But men managed before that date, didn't they, Ali? They lived. They talked. They played – without football.'

'Yes, but . . .'

'But nothing. Listen to me. Are you listening to me?'

'Yes.'

'They weren't any less manly, any less in touch with

37

their fathers or any less happy. Perhaps, in fact, they were happier.'

'Yes, although judging from the portraits of those times, you'd be hard pushed to prove it.'

'What?'

'Well, the men never smile in those portraits. They always have that stern look which says, "I'm a wealthy man who knows he will die of tuberculosis . . ."'

'. . . or rickets . . .'

'". . . Or rickets. And who is still waiting for someone to come up with the distraction from the woes of this life that is football."'

'You can't simply put the fact that men look happier now than they did in pre-Industrial Revolution portraiture down to the advent of football!'

'No, but maybe football *has* made men happier. It certainly distracts them from the sadness of life – and rickets.'

'Ali, that's just rubbish. Most men are made unhappy by football! My friend Jenny says she checks the football results at the weekend before going to work on a Monday to see what sort of mood her boss is likely to be in.'

'Who does he support?'

'I don't know. Sunderland, I think.'

'Trust me, he's generally going to be in a bad mood. She doesn't need to check the papers.'

'And how childish is that?! That the result of a football match, one silly football match, can change the mood of a man, a grown man with a proper job and a family, for days afterwards. The whole thing is childish. And, by dint of that association with your childhood, a part of you – that football part of you – will always be a small boy. And that's not good.'

'Why not?'

'Oh, God! Because a part of you will always be frozen in time, always wanting to return to the paternal womb.'

Ali was quiet.

'Which is, of course, impossible,' I added, in case he thought my poetic image was based on a truth I'd read somewhere as a girl while he was busy collecting football stickers. 'Even for a seahorse.'

'What?'

'The male seahorse carries the baby and therefore *does* have a paternal womb. You probably knew that. It's a beautiful thing.'

'I didn't, actually,' he says.

'Well, if you'd read the *Ladybird Book of the Sea* when you were younger, maybe you would.'

'I've got to go. I've got a radio job.'

'I'm trying to wean you! I've got a whole twelve-step programme and everything,' I lied.

'I know. It's a nice idea, Ronni, but . . . I've got to go. I'm late!'

And off he went, his little bald spot bobbing away down the street. A child in a man's body. The bald spot had got a lot bigger since we were together. In fact, years ago, Ali had told me he was thinking of converting to Judaism – not for any religious reason but just so that he could wear a skullcap and cover his bald spot. Now, years later, a skull cap might not be enough; he may need to become a Sikh if he is to satisfy his vanity.

That's it! Vanity! Alistair has always been a vain man. Well, he would say he 'takes a pride in his appearance' and likes to wear nice clothes. Your average man in the pub might even call him 'a dandy'. Or worse. Suffice to say, appearance matters to him. So I need to make Ali see that it's unattractive to follow football. Unattractive, unbecoming and childish.

I need to tell him my new thoughts before he goes cold on the whole idea.

'Ronni?'

'It's me!'

'I know.'

'How did you know?'

'Your number comes up . . .'

'Oh, yes.'

'I'm walking to the Tube; I'll be underground in a second.'

'Oh. Well, listen to me. Are you listening?'

'Yes, but I think I might disappear in . . .'

'You know how you once said to me that it's good to keep the child in us alive? To have a sense of wonder and innocence . . .'

'Did I?'

'You said it's what makes comedians funny: the inner child. It's what makes actors interesting, you said. It's what makes artists able to sit and paint.'

'Did I say that?'

'Yes. "We all need to play," you said.'

'I must write that down; it makes me sound very intelligent.'

'Yes. I think it was your excuse for going off to play five-a-side football instead of going out for a meal with me and my parents.'

'Oh.'

'Anyway, I was just thinking that you keeping the child alive doesn't mean you have to be stuck in the past. It doesn't mean you have to be a child or condone childish-ness.'

'Have I rung my daily horoscope?'

'What I'm saying is, do you really want to watch the likes of Wayne Rooney and John Terry kicking lumps out of each other and then shouting at the referee like overtired six-year-olds being told it's bedtime?'

'Have you got tickets to the Chelsea–Man U game?'

'No! Figuratively! Is that what you really want to see? To watch? Childishness? Petulance? Anger? Is it seemly to watch tens of thousands of men shouting at someone who used to play for their team and who has just dared to score for the opposition?'

Ali was quiet. He was either thinking or he'd been run over.

'Do you really want to be associated', I continued, 'with a gang of overweight, badly dressed men as they taunt another gang of overweight, badly dressed men for having done nothing but be born thirty miles down the road from them – in a town just as crappy as theirs?' I knew this was a bit strong (and not all football fans are like that) but I wanted to rile him.

He said nothing. Either I was eating away at his self-image or, I thought, he really had been run over. But surely I'd have heard something: a squeal of brakes, the scream of a passer-by . . .

'Piggy-faced men', I said, 'who pretend to be as tough as nails and then sit crying with their piggy-faced little children when their team gets relegated . . . It's playground behaviour, isn't it?' This I felt was actually pretty accurate, however.

'You're right.' Thank God, he was alive!

'I just think you need to take a good, hard look at your-self . . .' I said, although, thinking about it, I realise he already does – for an hour every morning, in a full-length mirror usually.

'Ali, do you really want to look like the men behind the goal? With hatred in their faces, their screwed-up adult-child faces?'

More silence.

'Okay, Ronni. It'll be difficult. But I'll do it. I'll . . . I'll give up football – for a year. I'm just going underground . . . Will it make me fat, though?'

'What?'

'When people give up smoking they get fat. Will it make me fat?'

'It won't make you fat!'

'I'm going underground . . .'

And he was gone. I'd lost his little voice but I'd got his little mind. Vanity, thy name is Alistair!

6

The First Cracks in the Armour

When I applied to go to Leeds University, I'd changed my allegiances from Leeds United to Coventry City. It's a shocking admission. Men aren't meant to change their football clubs. You can change your wife or your girlfriend and not suffer the taunts of your mates. They won't disown you for that. But your football club? Well, you just don't, do you? It's like changing your mother.

But I still hoped beyond hope that I'd get in to Leeds because (a) I liked it, (b) I didn't want to end up in Sheffield, and (c) because of the connection with Leeds United.

As you approach Leeds on the train, you pass the ground: Elland Road. The first time I saw it in 1982, as I went for my interview, I almost fainted with delight. There it finally was: this huge part of my youth finally in front of my very eyes. It was like seeing Narnia or Uncle Quentin's house – or Stuart Hall.

But while it was still the home of Leeds United, my old heroes were long gone. It was like looking at a house that you'd once lived in. The memories remained but there were new occupants now; it wasn't the same. Looking at Elland Road from the slowing train, I started to feel like the ghostly couple in *Beetlejuice*.

As I began my English degree at Leeds that first October, however, my mind was on more intellectual and romantic pursuits. Football had slipped down the list a little bit.

But only a little bit. It was still in third place. I was still jour-
neying from boyhood to manhood.

I'd decided to stay in halls, for the first year at least.
Devonshire Hall was an all-boys hall 'run along the lines of
an Oxford college', according to the slim accommodation
list. There was a quad, wooden doors, stone staircases,
gowns and boards to be worn for Sunday lunches – and
shared rooms.

I'd never shared a room. I'd been to an ordinary (good)
comprehensive in Evesham and only ever met people from
public school when I played tennis against teams from
Malvern.

When I arrived on that first Sunday evening, I remember
looking at the battered trunk (how old-fashioned, I thought,
was that?) sitting in the middle of the room under a pick-
up-sticks pile of tennis and squash racquets, hockey sticks
and skis. It looked like something out of a St Trinian's film.
To whom did it belong? I wondered. I went up to it and
prowled around it like a cat around a new item of furniture.
It had public-school boarder written all over it, and the
name 'Croft' printed on it. It sat like a bit of magician's kit in
the room; I half expected Master Croft to spring from it if I
got too close.

I realised there and then that I hadn't quite taken in the
idea of sharing a room. It was my mother's suggestion that
I should go to a boys-only hall – she thought girls were too
noisy and too distracting. Perhaps she'd realised how high
they had got on my list. 'Bigger than football?' – she knew
that this was something to be both impressed and frightened by.

There was no sign of 'Croft', so I thought I might as well
unpack. He had clearly chosen his side of the room. His

bed. Under the window – with the view of the tree.

I'd assumed that everyone, like me, would travel up or down to Leeds by train. But many of my fellow freshers had come in parental cars, laden with trunks, duvets, pot plants, stacking stereos and speakers.

Everyone wanted speakers in those days. They were touted on the street like drugs. I remember Scousers pulling up alongside you at random and opening van doors, saying, 'D'you want any speakers? They're good speakers, these, lad.' It's an odd phenomenon that back in the 1980s we wanted perfect sound from huge speakers; the bigger the speakers, the better the sound. Now we're happy to have the tinniest sound going as long as it comes from the tiniest thing. No self-respecting Marillion or Genesis or Spandau Ballet fan would have listened to their music via a mobile phone. I can only suppose The Saturdays sound better when you can't hear them so well.

Anyway, I took nothing other than my clothes on the train. And my 'luxury' items were: a personally typed list of Coventry City fixtures (with a space for each result), a homemade bar graph for goals scored by the Coventry players and my *Shoot!* League Ladders for the 1983–84 season.

In Mr Croft's absence, I unpacked my clothes and Blu-Tacked my stats proudly to the grey wall above my bed in my shared room. I even Blu-Tacked a pen to the side of the graph, such was my organisation and ongoing devotion to all things football.

When I met Richard Croft, he was clearly, as I had suspected, very used to the public-school atmosphere and to sharing a room. Within seconds, he had removed his shoes and socks and, while chatting to me, was clipping his toenails. If it was a territorial ploy – like a cat marking his territory with bodily fluids – it worked. I'd never seen anyone cut their toenails at quite such close proximity. At home, it was something we did in private. If this was what sharing a room would be like, I was rapidly going off the idea. To this day I have to avoid seeing anyone cut their toenails, otherwise I am plunged back into that fearful, hot-eared Sunday evening when I realised that my boyhood was behind me.

Richard was ahead of me with everything. He was a year older, with an assurance which I have come to realise is genetically part of anyone from Surrey, and had had 'a year out'. I'd never heard of this concept.

'A year out from what?' I asked.

It was an innocent query but became a joke Ronni and I would reprise twenty-one years later for a gag about Posh Spice wanting to take a year out and go travelling.

'I want to have a year out, David,' says Ronni's Posh.

'From what?' says my Beckham, alluding to her lack of career.

'From the education system,' said Richard, smartly. 'I didn't just want to go from school to sixth form to university to work. I thought I should see something of the world first.'

'Who'd do that?' I wondered.

'Everyone does it . . .'

Not when they were from Evesham they didn't.

'They normally go travelling. For a year.'

In 1983, spending a day in Wolverhampton was consid-ered an epic journey for anyone from Evesham. A journey from which the traveller might never return. You might even need jabs . . .

Richard told me he was an excellent squash player. I thought I was good – probably the best player of my age at the club in Evesham. Richard was ranked nationally.

He had arrived early and had already made friends. He even knew what the strangely bent coat hanger stuck on the front of the electric fire was for.

'Toast.'

'Toast?'

'Yeah. On Sundays they don't do an evening meal here.'

'Oh, yes. I think my mother said something about . . .'

'They just give out two slices of white bread per boy in the dining room between 5.30 and 5.45.'

'Right. That's pretty . . .'

'You come back and put it on the coat hanger in front of the gas fire. Tastes great; we used to do it at school.'

That explained the strong smell of toast I'd noticed half an hour previously as I had wandered down the long, creaky corridor trying despondently to find the room.

'Have you got any honey . . . ?'

'No. I'm more of a Marmite person.'

'Yuk!'

Those early days at Devonshire were among the unhappiest of my life. I felt completely out of place and began plotting my escape. You could only leave if you proved that you were undergoing serious psychological damage. I worked on it (like Corporal Klinger in *M*A*S*H*) and eventually proved it (by saying that the early hours didn't suit my work with Theatre Soc.). I was out of there before Christmas.

On the first Sunday, however – having missed breakfast,

47

which really was at some ridiculously early hour for any-one with an artistic bent (most of the other boys at Devon-shire were studying various sorts of engineering and chemistry) – I headed up to the JCR (Junior Common Room, apparently) where I had been told there lay Sunday papers.

Sunday papers meant one thing: football statistics – scores, attendances and league tables.

Under one arm, I carried my league ladders. Oh, the pleasure that was to come from updating them! It would be a touch of home, a touch of warmth, proof that I was alive – it's probably the equivalent of self-harming now.

The room was largely empty. I nodded at one of the other boys, who was deep in the financial pages. He looked at me suspiciously as I buried myself in all those football figures and facts. I drew out the time it took me to update the tables, savouring every minute of it – despite the frequent obtuse glances from my financial friend.

As I returned to the shared room, smiling and satiated, Richard looked at me.

'What is that under your arm?'

I paused. Caught like a thief.

'I've seen it on the wall above your bed. What *is* it?'

'My *Shoot!* League Ladders.'

'Your what whattie whatters?'

'Football league tables. You can move the teams' names around so that you always have an accurate version of the league tables.'

He looked at me blankly.

'Divisions one to four.'

He was more of a rugby and cricket man.

'And Scotland. Premier, one and two.'

He smiled as big a smile as it is possible to smile without laughing in someone's face.

'Isn't that the sort of thing you rather leave behind when you come to university . . .?'

I think it was a rhetorical question, but, in any case, I was so stunned I couldn't think of an answer. He shook his head, picked up his squash racquet, twirled it in his palm and left the room.

I knew then that perhaps it was time to stop updating my *Shoot!* League Ladders. Later that day, I tore down my graphs. And it hurt.

Brideshead Revisited had been shown earlier that year on ITV and had had a huge effect on all the students arriving at Leeds. There were teddy bears a-plenty and baggy trousers and open white shirts everywhere. I swear that a few people even affected stutters.

I'd loved the series myself, and so I entered into the *Brideshead* world of university life – there was no football in *Brideshead*.

Sebastian Flyte and Charles Ryder didn't ever sit around talking about Liverpool's rock-solid defence or the chances of Aston Villa and Ipswich Town breaking their stranglehold on English football.

Sebastian and Charles didn't read the league tables to each other in punts or chant football songs as they walked round the city of dreaming spires.

Sebastian and Charles didn't talk about who should or shouldn't be playing for England – they talked about quads not squads.

It was time to give up football. And for three years I did. More or less.

I'd gone to Leeds, to study English, and fell in with a

good crowd. We talked literature, we talked music, we talked arts, we talked films, we talked philosophy, we talked futures and pasts, we talked 'years out', we talked Nature, we talked curries, we talked politics (the miner's strike was happening just down the road and collections were commonplace in Leeds at that time), we talked sex, we talked about everything – except football.

I now refer to my student days as 'the wilderness years', during which nothing from the outside world really impinged on me. I lived in a bubble. We had no television in my student digs. I saw three films a week at the cinema but, for the first and only time, football didn't really play any part in my life.

Well, I still played twice a week. And cast the occasional glance at a newspaper. And went to a few matches in and around Yorkshire. But, compared to my total schoolboy absorption, it was 'prohibition'. In those days, if you 'more or less' gave up football, it was pretty easy to do so. There were no live TV games to speak of – except the FA Cup Final and the World Cup once every four years. There was no Radio 5 Live, no TalkSport, no Sky TV, no Champions League and no sports supplements in newspapers or glossy magazines other than *Shoot!*, which I'd now realised was really for under-eighteens.

If you wanted to know about football, you really had to work pretty hard. Other things entered my life.

Maybe Richard Croft had done me a favour.

Maybe Richard Croft had done Ronni a favour.

7

Early Doors . . .

Step Two: Give Up Match off the Day

Ali may have been dithering, but I know he'll see sense, and I have to be absolutely ready for him when he does. Ready and organised and prepared. All the things I find most difficult in the world. I have to concentrate. I have to come up with the goods. I have to really back up my words with actions. I have to be committed and see this through. It is not going to be easy for him; it is not going to be easy for me. But I have to make it look effortless. If he senses the slightest hesitation or uncertainty in me, he'll quit the programme. Ali likes organisation. And he likes lists. I once asked him, 'Why do you like lists so much, Ali?'

And he said, 'Because they make me feel:

(a) organised,

(b) hopeful, and

(c) calm.'

Organised, hopeful and calm: that's what I am right now. I've worked out my twelve-step programme and typed it up. It took a lot of time; I did it secretly while my husband was watching *Midweek Match of the Day*. He wondered why, for once, I wasn't nagging him about watching football. I didn't tell him it was because I was working out its total annihilation. I felt like a Bond villain; it was wonderful!

And here it is . . .

THE RONNI ANCONA TWELVE-STEP PROGRAMME TO WEANING YOUR MAN OFF FOOTBALL

(1) Find the root cause of the addiction to football ✓
(2) Give up Match of the Day
(3) Give up the Champions League
(4) Get him interested in other sports
(5) No more Monday-night football
(6) No more not-so-Super Sundays
(7) No more going to football games
(8) No more reading about it all in the papers
(9) No more watching England games – esp. 'friendlies'
(10) Take him to cultural events

As you can see, I only got to ten. But I am, as I've said, a great improviser; it will get finished.

There is a dull buzz on the entryphone. It can't be Ali, I think; it's before ten-thirty. He's never up early, especially when he's doing a theatre show. I open the door, and there he is in his cycling outfit.

'Okay, you're on! But I can't just give it all up at once though,' he says, wheeling his bike into my hall. 'The shock would be too great. I'd probably end up on the bathroom floor, sweating and twitching every Saturday at 10.30 at night – like that guy in *Trainspotting*.'

'Ewan McGregor.'

'Me and McGregor?'

'No, Ewan McGregor.'

'Me and McGregor?'

'Stop it!'

This is one of Alistair's favourite jokes. We tried – or *he* tried – to squeeze it into our Christmas Special in 2004. It didn't make the cut. I think out of damaged pride he is still trying to prove to me, five years on, that this stupid roundelay could have gone down in TV history. I couldn't believe I'd fallen into the vortex of his punning madness yet again.

'I think', says Ali, 'we need to work out some sort of programme.'

'Cold turkey?'

'Haven't you got any toast and Marmite?'

'No, I mean, like going cold turkey?'

'Oh. Yes, if you like . . .'

'That's why I have', I said, waving the slip of paper in front of him, '"The Ronni Ancona Twelve-Step Programme to Weaning Your Man Off Football."'

'Wow!'

'You didn't think I'd have a programme, did you?'

'No. That's . . . unusually organised of you.'

'Well, I've got to ten. I haven't quite finished it yet.'

'Right. Why don't you call it "The Ten-Step Programme to Weaning Your Man Off Football?"'

'Because it's always a Twelve-Step Programme.'

'Is it?'

'Yes. Always. I checked. I'm doing this properly, Ali. Scientifically. And in an organised way.'

'Good. Okay.'

We sit at my kitchen table. Ali wipes a crumb off with the edge of one hand into the waiting palm of the other and crosses the kitchen to put it in the bin.

'Have you finished?'

'Yes. A tidy kitchen is . . .'

'. . . impossible when you have two small children, Ali. Don't nag!'

'Right. So what's first . . .?'

'After finding the root . . .'

'Which we've done . . .'

'Which you've done, yes. Well done. A good start.'

'Thank you.'

'Not at all. After that . . . oh, look! It's *Match of the Day*.'

'No, no, no! That's going to be one of the hardest things! I can't start with that. Start me with something easy.'

'But I've typed it all up and everything.'

'Well, retype it! I can't go straight to *Match of the Day* – and there's only one "f" in "of" . . .'

'What?'

'You've written *Match off the Day*. It's "*of*" . . .'

'Give it back to me!'

I can see that I'm going to have to empower Ali – to make him think it's all his choice – even if it does mean retyping my list.

'So what do you want to start with?'

'I don't know, Ronni. It's your . . .'

'How about the Champions League?'

My husband is hooked on the Champions League. It seems like every bloody Wednesday I'm forced to hear that dreadful signature tune, which still sounds to me like someone singing 'La-sa-gna', and then I have to sit through a match between Manchester United and some foreign team in green from a place I've never heard of.

Step Three: Give Up the Champions League

I was living with Ali when the European Champions League began dominating Wednesday-evening television. To his credit, he tried to get me interested in this new interruption to my Wednesday night's TV.

He said, 'It's called the Champions League because it's for the individual champions of all the leagues in all the countries in Europe. It's like a reward for winning your league and a chance to see who are the best champions in Europe, the overall champions.'

I could just about see the logic of it. I wasn't interested, but it made some sort of sense.

'What particularly, apart from it being football, do you have against the Champions League?' asks Alistair.

'Well, for a start, apart from it being football, the teams in it are not all champions. Not any more. They can finish first in their leagues, yes. Or, according to my husband, they can finish second.'

'Or third.'

'Yes.'

'Or even fourth.'

'Yes, I know that, Ali. Fourth – and still qualify for (and even win) the so-called "Champions" League the follow-ing season.'

'As Liverpool did in 2005.'

'Yes. Thank you. The Champions League, it seems to me, is really just an excuse for the biggest, wealthiest, most famous teams in the biggest, wealthiest, most famous countries in Europe to play each other on TV every year in order to generate huge amounts of revenue and make sure that they remain the biggest, wealthiest and most famous teams and play each other again every year until the end of time in front of a TV audience of hundreds of millions. It's like *Eurovision* – without the songs, obviously.'

'Or the votes.'

'Yes.'

'Or the campery.'

'Yes.'

'Or Terry Wogan.'

'Yes.'

'So nothing like *Eurovision*, really.'

'All right, it's the football equivalent of *Groundhog Day*.'

'Without Bill Murray.'

'Yes.'

'Or . . .'

'Stop it, Ali! You're being really annoying today!'

'Well, I'm under attack, aren't I? My life is about to be eaten away.'

'No! Your life is about to be enriched. You're about to be set free from your football shackles. Listen to me. Are you listening to me, Ali?'

'Yes,' he says, grumpily.

'Nowhere else in football is there such an elitist, in-yer-face, exclusive little club as the Champions League. It is a behemoth of capitalism.'

'But, Ronni, the football's *really* good!'

'It's wealth out of control.'

'I can't give up the Champions League!'

'It's blatant showing off.'

'I didn't think it would all be this quick!'

'A members' club par excellence.'

'That you'd go this big so soon . . .'

'It's everything that most football fans hate.'

'No, it's everything we love!'

'Well, it's gone.'

'What?'

'The Champions League for you, Ali, is history. Live games. Highlights. The works. Now you'd better go and get on with your day. Your new life! Smile! It's all going to be great!'

'Is this what's going to happen, then? What it's going to be like?'

'You don't want to be dull for ever, do you?'

'I think that's a bit . . .'

'Good. Now go. I've got to make dinner for my husband.'

'It's eleven in the morning!'

'He's having some friends round tonight to watch the football . . .'

'How come you're not stopping Gerard from watching football?'

'. . . and I promised I'd cook something special . . .'

'What? Overcooked spaghetti and underflavoured bolognaise?'

'Excuse me! I do all sorts of nice things now. Although, as it happens, I am doing spaghetti tonight.'

'Well, if you put it on now, it should be ready by tonight.'

'Ali!'

'What day is it today, then?'

'Wednesday.'

'Oh, shit! I've got a matinee!'

And he was gone in a blur of Lycra and leg. Ali never forgot anything. I was unsettling him already.

8

Bye, Bye, Crewe!

Walking home from *Cabaret* that night, past the pubs all proclaiming that they'd had live Champions League football on offer, I remember how I used to enjoy the European Cup. The European Cup was the forerunner of the Champions League, and it was a knockout competition from the start.

In fact, the first game of football I remember watching was the 1971 European Cup final between Ajax of Amsterdam and Panathinaikos of Athens. I was six, and my father had hysterics listening to me trying to pronounce the names of both teams, forcing me to say them again and again as he chuckled away behind a cloud of pipe smoke. Indeed, in the way that family jokes last way beyond their sell-by date, he'd always say, 'Panathinaikos, eh, Al?' any time the team was mentioned over the following thirty-three years.

Before so many overseas players came to ply their trade in England, the European club tournaments were a chance to see how English teams with English players fared against French teams with French players, against German teams with German players. But now, thinking about it, the Champions League and UEFA Cup are totally meaningless as a litmus test of how England might perform against a European national side. There is no romance. No mystery. It's like watching stags fighting.

I reach home and put my key in the door. Once inside,

I'm tempted to break the silence of the flat by putting on the television. It would be so easy. She wouldn't know. Just one more Champions League highlights programme wouldn't hurt, would it?

But the Champions League . . . Ronni's right. It's the height of capitalism; it is everything football fans should react to, but they don't. Well, I will!

For a start, there's the ads . . .

For years, I'd not taken much notice of the pitch-side advertising hoardings, until I started watching the Champions League. Then, suddenly, one year, the adverts started to move; it was like watching a Pixar movie. The ads danced, they jumped, they proclaimed, across European boundaries, the dubious benefits of Coca-Cola and McDonald's and Goodyear tyres. They were screaming out, 'Look at all us big companies, the polluters, the exploiters. Here we are!'

Suddenly, anyone with half a brain could see that this is what the Champions League is all about. Business. Big business, multinational business. Globalisation par excellence.

And the biggest joke of all: the dancing adverts now draw so much attention to themselves that they are frequently more agitated than the players, more interesting than the game.

Then there's the environmental impact . . . When we're all being urged to consider our carbon footprint, the very sport that could reach millions with an environmental message wants to carry on as if nothing is happening. If the teams have to travel, let them travel, I suppose. But when the game is on television anyway, should we still be encouraging 5,000 people on 150 planes to fly from

Manchester and Liverpool and London to Barcelona and Milan and Munich to cheer their team on in the Capitalists League?

Besides, when they get to the city, the venue for the match, do any of the fans actually do anything in that city apart from drink from jugs and dance in fountains? If you're going to Barcelona, surely you'd want to see the beauty of its buildings, feel the quaintness of the Ramblas and be moved by the art of Picasso and Miró, wouldn't you?

If you were in Milan, surely you'd want to walk on the roof of the Duomo, see La Scala, wander slowly through the fashion quarter, wouldn't you?

And in Munich . . . Well, okay. In Munich you might just go for the football and come back.

And if the European League (for that's what it is) is here to stay, then what next? What price a World League in ten years' time? And the members' club gets smaller. And the journeys get longer. And the world gets hotter. African clubs. South American clubs. Indian clubs beamed into our homes like anaesthetic. Bye-bye, Crewe. And Luton. And Northampton. The walk to the ground, the local derby, the friendly rivalry will be a thing of the past. The rich will get richer. The champions will continue to be champions win or lose. All thanks to the Champions League. If you keep watching it, the behemoth will continue to grow and spread its mighty, sponsored wings.

Do I want to be responsible for the death of local football? The football I grew up with? No! Do I still want to watch the Champions League? Yes!

The phone rings.

'Did you watch it?'

'No, Ronni.'

'Not even a glimpse at work?'

'No.'

'And you're not going to watch the highlights?'

'No. Nothing.'

'Good. Well done. I'm proud of you.'

'I mean, you're right about the "behemoth of capitalism" bit. I'd thought it for a long time but couldn't actually bring myself to stop watching it. I suppose you've done me a favour, Ronni. I've taken the first step on a long, hard road.'

'That's brilliant! This is going to be so good for you, Ali!'

'Did Gerard watch it?'

'Yes.'

'What was the score?'

9

'Easy! Easy!'

I'm trying not to gloat about how easy that was. It was like Ali had always been trying to give up the Champions League but hadn't been able to actually say to anyone how much he had gone off it. I was like some sort of therapist. I just had to get him to admit more of his feelings, to formulate the doubts he's clearly been having for some time. Maybe I should get a couch and a box of tissues for all the men who would follow Ali to my house to partake in my programme. And frame some certificates. Okay, they would be ballet certificates and not from the Royal College of Psychiatrists, but no one would notice when I'd hypnotised them or got them all bleary-eyed as they confessed that they only liked football in the first place in order to please their overbearing fathers and only carried on liking it to avoid being dropped by their mates, or being called 'dandies' – or worse . . .

Maybe, all football fans are like this, scared to own up to any of their friends that really, deep down, the product is tarnished, that they are no longer in love with it. They can't admit it to their wives or they'll lose the possibility of using football as a refuge, but perhaps the love affair is over and they're too scared to admit it. Football really is like any other girlfriend . . .

As my husband once said to me, 'Where relationships are concerned, most men don't get out of the shower until the bath is running.'

'What?' I said in reply, shocked at his sudden ability to talk about relationships from a male point of view – and his ability, indeed, to talk for a second about anything other than football.

'They don't', he said, 'leave their failing relationship until a new one has begun with someone else.'

'Oh, good. I'm glad they don't actually have the water running in the shower and the bath; that would be a hideous waste.'

'I suppose so,' he said, as he went back to reading the football reports in the paper.

But how typical of men not to own up to the end of a relationship. Until something better comes along, they'll stick with it. Weakly. Deceptively. Opportunistically. Sadly, nothing comes along to replace football. Unless I can open men's eyes and show them that there are other things to watch, other things to do.

Yes, I must show Ali other things. If there is now a gap in his week and in his mind which I have created by freeing him from watching roughly seven hours of Champions League football every week, I have to fill that time or he'll soon slip back into his old ways. Where's my list? Didn't I have 'a programme' somewhere? Maybe I could ask Ali to go for a walk. Ummm . . . that's a tough one – generally men and walks don't go. At least, the concept of strolling is anathema to most men I have ever known. The conversation normally goes something like this:

'Shall we go for a walk?'

'Where to?'

'Just out somewhere.'

'But where to?'

'Just out, I don't know.'

'Are we meeting someone?'

'No, I just thought we could go for a walk.'

'But where to?'

'Our usual little route.'

'Are we trying to beat our record?'

'It's just a walk!'

'I'm happy here. There's football on soon.'

Hopefully, Ali will be different. He likes nature and he likes exercise. I call him.

'Do you want to come for a walk with me?'

'Where to?' he says.

'Just out somewhere.'

'But where to?'

'Just out, I don't know.'

'Are we meeting someone?'

'No, I just thought we could go for a walk.'

'But where to?'

'Our usual little route.'

'Are we trying to beat our record?' he says.

'It's just a walk!'

'I'm happy here. There's football on soon.'

'I hope you haven't been watching any Champions League football!'

'No, it's going okay actually, Ronni. I'm managing without that. I've started eating more, definitely, to make up for it, but I'm coping so far.'

'It's only been four days.'

'Well, even so . . .'

'What have you been doing instead?'

'Watching the snooker.'

'Well, it's something, I suppose.'

'Ronnie O'Sullivan is a genius.'

'All right. Forget the walk. I'll see you tomorrow for step four of your programme.'

'What is step four?'

'You'll find out tomorrow!'

'You've lost your list, haven't you?'

'No . . .'

'Why don't you just give me the list next time for safe keeping?'

'That's not the way these things work! I need to monitor you step by step,' I said, also knowing that if Ali saw the steps in blue and white, the whole idea would be too much for him.

But what was step four? I know I had a list somewhere. Where was it? Ah, under the unfinished bowl of Coco Pops, of course. Aha! Step Four: 'Get him interested in other sports . . .'

IO

'City Till I Die'

I couldn't have been a bigger Leeds fan. I knew the age and height and birthplace of every player; I knew the price of every plastic-smelling item on offer in the club shop, from comb cases to programme holders, from 'pendants' (50p plus p&p) to 'ladies pants with club motif' (£1.25 plus p&p). But something changed. The players (my heroes) left the club one by one as they aged. The team went downhill (yes, you could say I was a fair-weather fan). Geography and logic intervened.

Some people would go so far as to call me a traitor. A deserter. It's not done – 'United till you die.' But I changed.

My father and I spent the 1970s going to a game a month. As I've said, we always saw Leeds if they were playing within a thirty-five-mile radius of Evesham. But we'd turn up to any number of other games at Villa, West Brom and . . . Coventry.

The road to Coventry was easy. We went via Stratford-on-Avon. The parking was good, the ground was easy to find and always felt friendly. We started to go more and more often and got to know the team and the players. Before I knew it, I could feel myself drifting away from Leeds. I knew what I was doing was wrong, but when the last of the players from my era, the Don Revie era, had left the club, I found myself one day buying a sky-blue Coventry City scarf from the sky-blue Coventry City shop and, one by one, the sky-blue items of the Coventry City kit. I put them on and looked in the mirror. They felt good.

I was in love with another club.

One of the other things that had put me off Leeds was the crowd trouble. The late 1970s and early 1980s was one of the worst times for crowd trouble, and while Leeds United may have been slipping down the First Division table, their fans were resolutely stuck at the top of the football-violence table, right up there with Manchester United, Chelsea and Millwall. The Big Four. The Hard Four.

Coventry didn't have any hardcore trouble-making fans; Coventry, in fact, had very few fans at all.

After one game, ironically at Coventry (which, for the first time, my mother and sister, Kay, had come to), we had found ourselves pinned to a wall outside the ground as about two hundred of my fellow Leeds fans, scarves and flares billowing in the late-summer breeze, tore down the street chased by a score of policemen and horses. The backdraught of the running mob nearly took my face off. Surprisingly, Mum was the least troubled of all of us. She has always been disturbed by the most unusual things. She's always, for example, had a particular hatred of farting. Farting of any sort. Public. Private. Farting on television. Farting in film.

If she's ever watching a movie with me or my sister, we might worry about the sex or the violence being unsuitable for a gently-mannered woman in her mid-seventies. In fact, she's fine with any amount of shooting, swearing or skin on skin, but she can't bear the least reference to farting. Mel Brooks's *Blazing Saddles* would possibly induce lockjaw in her.

So that day at Coventry in August 1977, she was not perturbed by the marauding hordes in yellow, white and blue as they roared past us. Had any of them broken wind as they ran, however, it would have been a different story; the schoolteacher in her would have sided with the police and she'd have been pulling those young lads into the station by the scruffs of their sweaty, northern necks.

My father, sister and I, however, were terrified, saddened and ashamed.

It was not the first time I'd seen trouble around a Leeds match. Over the seasons, I'd watched and read, damned by association, endless news reports about Leeds fans causing damage to towns, trains and people around the country. And I'd had potentially the best night of my young football-supporting life doubly ruined by the Leeds fans who ran riot after Leeds United had been cheated out of the European Cup final in Paris in 1975.

I've never understood the fighting gene – with or without football.

On another occasion I was walking down Oxford Street as a child on a family visit to London's theatreland. Suddenly, I heard the sound of raised, chanting voices – which I associated with football fans and Alsatians on the TV news. I was filled with fear. The chanting was rhythmic. There were even drums.

In the distance, I could see people fanning out to let this chanting group pass and, judging by the shape of the fan, these people were coming my way. They seemed to have their heads shaved like skinheads. The noise got louder. Who did they support and what were they going to do to me? To us? And then my mum said to me, 'It's okay. It's the Hare Krishnas.'

I didn't know what that meant. I do now – sort of. But, back then, they frightened me. Every time we came to London they seemed to be around with their drums and bells and chants; it was years before I realised they were peaceful!

And once, irony of ironies, as they passed us on one side, a trio of Manchester United fans passed us on the other. They cast a contemptuous glance at these young men, in their billowing, pastel-orange robes, chanting in unison, slaves to their beliefs.

'Look at those idiots, all dressed the same, chanting that rubbish. What a bunch of poofs!'

And then, without any sense of irony, they set off, like a rival group of birds in a rainforest, chanting, 'U-ni-ted! U-ni-ted! U-ni-ted!'

Football fans somehow seem to see themselves as doing something noble. Belonging. Belonging together. And so, like medieval warriors, they defend the honour of their town, their club, the generations of fans who have behaved just as badly as they have over the last decades. I've never really had that sense of belonging or of needing to belong to any one group.

So I started going to see Coventry regularly with my dad. I soon had the autographs of most of their players and knew their ages and heights and birthplaces. Coventry City in the early 1980s were never as good as Leeds had been in their heyday – few teams ever could be – but they became ours. Mine and Dad's. We helped to pay their wages with our ticket money and my endless purchases of needless souvenirs (but never the 'ladies pants with club motif') from the club shop.

I suppose I've always felt I was two people in one – or more. Maybe it's a subconscious result of being partly

Anglo-Indian. Perhaps I'm not anything 'till I die' except 'me', and football, like Leeds United, was just a stage. Football was the young me. I don't have to take it with me through life.

I used to like eating Space Dust, but you go off things. You leave them behind.

Am I really thinking this? Maybe Ronni's 'Ten/Twelve-Step Programme' isn't going to be hard work at all. Maybe it will expand me as a person. Maybe it's actually going to be easy. Maybe . . . I'm going to miss it like mad.

Football Is a Giant Ant

Step Four: Get Him Interested in Other Sports

If, by now, you've convinced the man in your life that he should grow out of football and made him even half-aware that he doesn't want to look like the men behind the goal and convinced him of the corporate evils of the Champions League, perhaps angle his competitive instincts towards other sports. But be careful . . .

GOLF

Golf is not a good idea. Golf is more time-consuming televisually than football. When it's on, it's on for hours at a time for days at a time. Oh, and Gary Lineker presents that too. So if wanting to see the back of Crisp Boy is one of your chief desires in all this, suggesting golf to your bloke as a substitute for football isn't going to help anybody.

It would be even worse if he were to take up the sport. Golf always takes hours and happens several times a week. And the people involved are uniformly dull. They may not be as loutish as the average footballer and are arguably better dressed (if you like Pringle patterns), but golfers really can bore for their country and will make you yearn for the smell of mustard and frothy urine within twenty minutes of being in their company.

CRICKET

Cricket too is a danger. Again it can take hours at a time for days at a time on television. And the noise of a cricket crowd is every bit as annoying as the noise of a football crowd: the supporters seem to have simply copied a number of football chants and, in between those chants, keep up a dull hum of drunkenness which, as it seeps through your surround-sound speakers, only makes you think the fridge is malfunctioning.

Nothing ever seems to happen, and I've always thought cricketers must be mad anyway. For a start, they have that huge, great, green, lush pitch and choose to play on that tiny parched little postage stamp in the middle. What a waste of space! Why don't they play lots of games at the same time? Or rent out the outfield for arable farmland?

RUGBY UNION

Men who like football tend not to like rugby. It's a class thing – certainly with rugby union anyway. So it's probably not even worth trying to get him interested. You'll have to buy him a whole new wardrobe too, with striped pastel shirts, black brogues and orange corduroy trousers. Okay, rugby matches are ten minutes shorter, and the players are so hunky it might encourage your other half to work out a bit more. There are also fewer televised matches, but they are traditionally watched in very loud, very posh, very drunken groups. So, unless you want your living room to be inundated with loads of beer-swigging rugger-buggers with jumpers slung round their necks and their shirt collars up, it's best to keep away from the oval ball.

FORMULA I

No! No! No! Just the noise of it will drive you mad. And how can you trust a sport in which the aim is simply to go round in circles quickly? And all that wasted fuel; if they are all going in the same direction, couldn't they at least give each other a lift?

SNOOKER

Snooker can be very dull. It is extremely reliant on the players' charisma, which isn't a great thing, as they generally don't have any. And it goes on for ever; the same picture of the green table filling the screen. In fact, when I was younger I used to mistake it for the 'test card'. I thought it was an alternative to the long-haired girl doing noughts and crosses.

In a desperate attempt to make the proceedings more interesting, the commentators always seem to speak in a hushed growl, which just makes snooker sound like a very long Carlsberg commercial.

But there is some fun to be had trying to work out who the palest player is. The poor things never see the sunshine and all look as if they are severely vitamin-D deficient.

BOXING

Although boxing is a very masculine sport, it has quite a neurotic element about it. It seems to me that the boxers are always obsessing about their weight. There is a whole plethora of categories for them to get paranoid about: flyweight, bantamweight, lightweight, welterweight, middleweight, heavyweight, what a weight, can't weight . . . for another chocolate biscuit.

They even have a weigh-in before the fight to see if they can actually do their job. Imagine that at any other place of work. It would be terrifying! 'Sorry, you're two pounds too heavy to come to work today, Mr Holmes.'

Although it can be impressive to watch, it is not exactly going to encourage your other half to get in touch with his feminine side. And I've always thought how disappointing it must be to go through all that dancing around in your pants and getting hit on the nose only to win a big belt. Which they never seem to get to wear out. Probably just as well – they'd only get teased and get into a fight.

AMERICAN FOOTBALL

Don't even think about going all-American on him. American football is as likely to catch on here as the cowboy hat. Or Reece's Peanut Butter Cups. Or *Joey*.

And as for baseball, it's always on too late at night. It's unfathomable. And even girls acknowledge it's just rounders in trousers.

No. Your best bet is tennis.

TENNIS

Tennis only really happens in this country for two weeks a year: Wimbledon. It may be wall-to-ivy-covered-wall coverage for that time, but compared to the forty-six weeks (or is it fifty-two?) of football every year, two weeks of tennis is surely a sacrifice worth making. The sheer psychological battle of a tennis match – one mind pitted against another – with all its ups and downs and twists and turns and 'Come on, Andy!'s, is surely enough to get anyone hooked (with a little gentle persuasion).

And the one-on-one, winner-takes-all battle is easy to sell as superior to the eleven-against-eleven-ooh-I-might-just-have-a-breather-and-hide-out-on-the-wing-for-a-bit tedium of a football match.

But tennis isn't hyped in the same way as football. It's not in your face and down your throat and round every corner. It's a seasonal fruit – like Wimbledon's famous strawberries. Football is now a year-round, preservative-filled giant plum.

I know I can't lure Alistair further away from football with tennis because it simply isn't prolific enough to satisfy his sporting cravings, but I can lure him with that kind of fruit-based politics.

I call him again.

'What is it now, Ronni?'

'I just thought of something else about football . . .'

'Can we talk later? Ronnie O'Sullivan's on for a 147 . . .'

'. . . how it destroys everything in its path.'

'Does it?' He sounded completely disinterested.

'Yes, it swallows up all the other little sports. It's not fair. Quite frankly, I am amazed that a hobby is so indulged by a whole nation. If football were a religion, there would be uproar that other religions were not being shown the same respect or given the same airtime.'

'But, Ronni, people have an appetite for football that no other sport can match. Or could match. That's why it's so exposed; it's really popular!'

'Maybe if those other little sports had half the exposure that football gets, they would be more popular.'

'Come on, Ronnie!'

'Come on what?'

'I was talking to Ronnie O'Sullivan.'

'Oh. But you don't want other sports to die, do you, Ali?'

'Well, maybe cricket.'

'Yes, well, maybe cricket. But other sports that you also love are being killed off by football. Football is like the big grey squirrel that's killing off all the little red squirrels that are the other, minor sports.'

'Go on . . .'

There was a note of hesitancy in his voice. Either he was bending or he was trying to work out my poorly expressed red-squirrel imagery.

'What are you saying, Ronni?'

I'd got him! As I've said, Ali loves nature and would do anything to protect any animal that was endangered. Unless it was the clothes moth. They eat his clothes. Ali likes his clothes. He hates the clothes moth. And kills them – regularly. His flat is, in fact, peppered with little smeary marks – the papery remains of scores of dead clothes moths. Oh, and he keeps his most precious clothes in the freezer. It kills the moth eggs, apparently. You see, while in some ways Ali is a typical football fan, in other ways he is madder than me.

'Don't you remember, Ali, years ago when we watched the Olympics together . . .?'

'1996. Atlanta.'

'Yes. 1996. Well, remember how many sports you enjoyed watching during the Olympics? How exciting you said badminton was, for example?'

'Yes . . .'

Every four years it comes as a surprise to us all, but somehow it's true: badminton is brilliant! Okay, when played by four geography teachers in a village hall, it's not great to watch – or play. But actual international badminton rocks! It's quick. It's skilled. It's full of variety and touch and it doesn't look that difficult.

'Go on, Ronni!'

'Which one?'

'You!'

'Oh. And remember how you said, "It's a pity such minority sports don't get more television and newspaper coverage at other times of the sporting year" . . .'

'Did I?'

'Yes, you did. And I said, "That's because they're all obsessed with football."'

'Yes, you did.'

'And basketball. We watched that too at the Olympics in Atlanta that year and you said, "How exciting a sport is basketball!"'

'No, I didn't.'

'You did, Ali.'

'I wouldn't have said that.'

'But you did.'

'No. It's such a badly structured sentence. I might have said, "Isn't basketball exciting?" Or, "I didn't realise how exciting basketball is." But I would never have said, "How exciting a sport is basketball!" It's an American phrasing; I hate it.'

'Stop picking hairs.'

'Splitting.'

'What?'

'It's splitting hairs.'

'Well, whatever it is, you liked the basketball . . .'

'So did you.'

'Yes. Because they kept scoring baskets! Not like silly football, where you can watch a game for an hour and a half and still no one's scored a goal!'

'A nil–nil can be fantastically exciting!'

'Ummm, fantastically . . .'

'It can be if you really . . .'

'And rowing. We loved watching it at the Olympics. And, again, I remember how you said, "Why is rowing so exciting?" And I said, "Because it's not football."'

'Ronnie, Ronnie, Ronnie! You're a bloody genius!'

'Thank you. I know!'

'I meant Ronnie O'Sullivan.'

'Oh, will you turn that off!'

'Ronni, I can watch snooker and still listen to you.'

'Turn it off!'

'Oh, all right! It's off!'

'Is it?'

'You can't hear it, can you?'

'Are you sure it's off and not on mute?' Because I . . .'

'It's off!'

'Ali . . .?'

'Oh, all right! There. It's off.'

'Well, I hope it is off and not on stand-by because you always say that that's a waste environmentally and you wouldn't want to be a . . .'

'Ronni! It's off! I've even pulled the plug out! Now get on with your fucking point!'

'Ali!'

'Well, why you couldn't have told me while . . .'

'Listen to me. Are you listening to me, Ali?'

'Yes!!!'

'Good. Now, listen. Football is killing all these little

sports. Don't you see? Just like Morrisons and Tesco's are killing off the corner shops.'

Ooh, another silence!

Ali doesn't like that. That hits home even deeper than the squirrels. Ali likes the corner shops. Supports them. He actually stood in the street next to me once with a placard on a demo, shouting, 'Keep our lo-cal shops! I said, Keep our lo-cal shops!' to the tune of 'Oops, Upside Your Head'. Okay, on that occasion it wasn't actually out of sympathy for Raj and Suri Patel and their dusty business of twenty-five years' standing but because he didn't want to have to go any further for his newspaper (and the football results and reports contained therein) but . . . it's still got be worth pointing out the parallel. I try again.

'Football is killing the minority sports. Eating them up like a . . . giant ant with big teeth and huge jaws – and an unusual appetite for minor sporting activities.'

'I agree. But what can you do?'

'What can you do? You can stop watching it and watch other sports instead!'

'I was! I was watching the snooker.'

'Oh, yes. Well, that's good.'

'Can I put it back on then?'

'In a minute, yes. And get used to watching it, Ali. Because soon you won't be watching *any* football.'

'So I've got to give up watching *entirely*?'

'In time, yes. Of course.'

There is a strangled noise from the other end of the phone. Either Ali is finding this hard to take or he has stood on a staple.

'You'll be helping the survival of endangered sports.'

'Yes, but . . .'

'You want to see this through, don't you?'

I knew Ali never gave up: he never liked to be seen as a quitter. He didn't know it but he had given me my two biggest weapons in all of this: his pride and his commitment.

'Okay. So what's next?'

'Monday-night football.'

'What?!'

'Come to me tomorrow . . .'

Elland Road Visited

That night, I lay in bed staring at the ceiling, with the songs from *Cabaret* going round in my head in the way they always do when you're in a musical; little snatches from this number and that number. Sometimes you're only half aware that your other nocturnal thoughts are being under-scored by bits from 'Wilkommen' and 'Two Ladies' and 'Tomorrow Belongs to Me'.

I'd thought about watching some more snooker but sud-denly that too had lost its lustre. The part is tiring, but tonight I lie sleepless.

'Tomorrow belongs to . . .' Certain of Ronni's pro-grammes I was happy to go along with, but suddenly the impending loss of another slice of football really hit me. What was I doing this for? 'Biddle-dee-biddle-dee-dee.' Okay, it was a challenge, but even though football had started to seem less and less a part of my life, it was still a part of me, wasn't it? Surely it always would be. 'Oh, Fatherland, Fatherland, show us the sign!'

As much as I'd tried to give it up at university in 1983, I couldn't. Richard Croft and Sebastian Flyte and Charles Ryder had taken me out of football but they couldn't take football out of me. 'Two ladies . . . and I'm the on-ly man, ja!' Maybe it was because I was in Leeds, though. The magic of that name: 'Leeds'. There was barely a day that went by from the time I went on holiday to Barmouth until the time I actually arrived at the university that I didn't say that name:

'Leeds'. Leeds United. Leeds University . . . 'Leeds, Leeds, Leeds!'

After a few weeks of settling in to university life and reluctantly learning to leave certain elements of football behind, it was time to pay proper homage. I'd seen the ground from the train a couple of times now. But I'd never been to Elland Road. My dad and I never got that far. It was October 1983, and Leeds United were playing Grimsby Town.

By that time, Leeds had been relegated to the Second Division and were not finding it easy to get out of. They were managed by Allan Clarke (their former centre-forward whose habit of holding onto the cuffs of his shirt I'd copied for years on and off the pitch – to the detriment of many a jumper), but all other connections with the team and the club of my childish childhood dreams had gone. Except that the Leeds number 7 that day in 1983 against the mighty Grimsby Town was Peter Lorimer.

Lorimer had been the player I'd most wanted to be. I remember asking my mother – not a keen seamstress – to stitch a nervous blue '7' on my precious white Leeds shirt in his honour. My favourite Scottish team was Dundee (birthplace of Peter Lorimer). If I could have changed my name to 'Peter Lorimer' by deed poll, I'd have done it.

Lorimer's right-foot shot had been measured – God knows how they did it in those days (perhaps by driving a Rover 3000 alongside the ball) – at over 90 miles an hour, faster even than the great Bobby Charlton's. I used to practise and practise and practise kicking the ball as hard as I could against the wall of the house, the side of the coal bunker, the chrysanthemums trying to be Peter Lorimer, forever commentating on my puny efforts in the style of David Coleman: 'Lorimeeeer – 1–0! 2–0! 3–0!'

I'd seen Lorimer play for Leeds around the Midlands in his heyday but I'd never seen him play at Elland Road. He was older now and heavier, but it still gave me a thrill to see him on his home turf (that famous Yorkshire turf) and to hear the fans shout 'Naine-teh mai-yuls an 'ow-wer' in a chorus of Leeds accents (an accent I was starting to adopt out of self-preservation) every time he lined up a free kick in homage to his '90-mile-an-hour' right foot.

I remember walking up the small hill to Elland Road that day with a lad called Rick from Chesterfield, who was also on my course and also at the 'Oxbridge-style' Devonshire Hall. Rick, like me, had chosen to put Leeds University on his UCCA form because of that famous Leeds United side. He'd grown up following them and, like me, had lapsed as Leeds faltered and the Revie boys left the club. We stood behind the goal that day like fallen angels returning to a former heaven to spy on their old God.

It was sad to see the once mighty Leeds labouring to beat Grimsby Town ('with all due respect to Grimsby Town', as they say). But there I was at Elland Road. I was finally there.

We'd taken the bus – the number 4 to Beeston – we'd stood, leaning on the crash barriers we'd seen in countless pictures of the famous empty ground, we'd stood in front of lads with the classic Leeds scarf – a white wool/nylon mix with an occasional horizontal yellow and blue stripe – knotted round their indigenous necks and wrists. This is what it must have been like for the people of Leeds while I was reading those results 250 miles away. This is how it felt.

Leeds won 3–0, Lorimer scored the final goal. I had a

fleeting hope that perhaps a new Leeds United would emerge; perhaps Rick and I would be part of the phenomenon while we were studying at Leeds University. Perhaps I would put Leeds and football first again – without the *Shoot!* League Ladders, obviously. Maybe Charles Ryder and Sebastian Flyte didn't know what they were missing; judging from the way they wore their jumpers slung round their necks, they probably liked rugby anyway.

I went to Elland Road again a couple of weeks later full of this new optimism, this time with my neat-nailed roommate, Richard Croft. Leeds were at home to Chelsea. Richard 'quite liked' Chelsea. We sat this time; Richard didn't want to stand. We had two slatted wooden seats high up in the main stand. From our lofty position we could see the game well; we could also see the road behind the stand behind the goal.

I'd once read that the fans who populated that area behind the goal went to the games at Elland Road with pinstripe suits on in order to look respectable, and then – like early versions of the Chippendales – would tear them off to reveal the jeans and bovver boots and pointless hatred of trouble-makers.

But there were no signs of any pinstripes that day. In fact, there were few signs of any fans behind the goal. Attendances nationwide were dwindling.

As we glanced at the road behind the stand, there were, however, a lot of 'fans' outside the ground – walking, milling, chanting. Then, suddenly, running, chasing, kicking and fighting: Leeds v. Chelsea. Before long there were policemen and dogs and vans. There were helmets on the floor, there were boots in groins and fists in faces. I'd seen trouble before, but nothing like this.

It was two hundred yards away but, with everyone behind standing up to watch, it felt like it was all around us. This was everything I'd come to hate about the game – about Leeds, about men. Sebastian and Charles won the day. I didn't go back to see any football for over two years. And I didn't go back to Elland Road for another fifteen. Leeds never got out of the Second Division while I was at university.

I nodded off to sleep and dreamt that Ronni was alternately Jeremy Irons and Anthony Andrews, punting me down the river under the weeping willows, past Don Revie and his famous eleven, who lay on grassy banks playing bingo, wearing candy-stripe blazers and waving us goodbye. Then Ronni was a giant ant, walking awkwardly all over us and singing 'Tomorrow Belongs to Me'. Badly.

13

'Sprouts Are Traditional . . .'

Step Five: No More Monday-Night Football

'Monday football' never used to exist. And it still doesn't as such. There is simply one game that is held over from the weekend to be played and shown live on a Monday night – just in case, after all the excitement of Saturday and Sunday, people have suddenly forgotten what football is.

This time, I go to Ali's flat for our therapy session. He is 'exhausted', he tells me, from his exertions on stage. Ali is always 'exhausted'; I tell him he should try having children! It's amazing how you manage to prepare breakfast, clear breakfast, crawl around as an imaginary horse with screeching little passengers on your back, build several Lego castles, try to persuade a distraught fairy princess that putting a pair of wellies on won't ruin her magical powers, walk around the park several times, try to persuade a distraught fairy princess that taking *off* a pair of wellies won't ruin her magical powers, bake several batches of mutant cupcakes, clear up the Lego, clear up the cupcakes, search for a small cloth rabbit, and it's still only 10 o'clock in the morning.

It's strange going to his flat and seeing little bits of our old life together. A desk we shared, a dresser that we bought together in Camden Market, a microwave that he was once given in lieu of payment for a job. Nice things that we used together and looked at together. And new things that he has bought which I would never have allowed in the house.

And everything so neat. Alistair has always been neat. He even *enjoys* tidying things up. He once told me how, as a boy, he'd always help his mum clean the house on a Saturday morning and so would deliberately mess his bedroom up on a Friday night to give himself more to do, so that he could make more of a difference. Ah! What a fool!

When we lived together, he always used to say, 'A tidy desk is a tidy mind.' I used to say, 'My desk's untidy; would you mind . . .?' And he'd clear my desk. But he couldn't clear my mind. Nothing can do that. Except for looking at a picture of the young Dustin Hoffman.

'So how are you getting on?' I ask, turning down the offer of a hot Ribena. 'I was really worried when the phone just went dead like that the other night.'

'So worried that you couldn't stop texting me to see if I was okay?'

'Well, all right. It's difficult when you have children. But I was concerned, that's all.'

'Umm . . .'

'I know this is difficult for you, Ali . . .'

'Well, that's . . .'

'And it's going to get a lot worse.'

'Right.'

'It has to.'

'Does it?'

'Yes. You've seen *Trainspotting*.'

'I haven't, actually.'

'But you know it. Ewan McGregor and . . .'

I see him take a breath.

'Don't start!'

'I wasn't going to do it!'

'Anyway, coming off an addiction hurts. You have to be really . . . are you listening to me?'

'Yes, I was just putting a few things away.'

'Leave it now.'

'I can do two things at once.'

'You can't. That's what women do. It's called . . . what's it called?'

'Multi-tasking.'

'Yes, multi-tasking. Stop cleaning!'

'Sorry!'

'Honestly! You're so anal.'

'Don't use that word.'

'It's Freud's word, not mine. Anyway, you are anal. Now, what was I saying?'

'That I have to be . . .'

'Oh, yes. You have to be dedicated and . . . Ali, can you turn that music off. I can't concentrate with that on. What is it anyway? It's terrible!'

'*Carousel*. It's . . .'

'Thank you. Now, looking at you, I think you're ready to move on to my next stage. As I said, giving up Monday-night football.'

'Yeah, I've been thinking about that . . .'

'It's got to go!'

'Not my Monday nights,' he begs, 'it's traditional. Couldn't I give up . . .'

'Don't start on the old "traditional" malarkey; it's only as traditional as the advent of Sky Television, which is what, ten years ago?'

'1979.'

'What?!'

'I heard it on 5 Live recently. 1979, it started. But they only started showing football in 1992.'

'There you are then. That's not that traditional, is it? Anyway, "traditional" is not always a good thing. Sprouts are traditional at Christmas, and we all know that they are the grapes of the devil.'

'Only you, Ronni, have that particular prejudice.'

'Anyway, it should be easy enough for now; you're on stage every Monday, aren't you?'

'Well, yes. But I Sky Plus the football and see it when I get home . . .'

'Not any more you don't.'

'But . . .'

'Do you want to do this or not, Ali?'

'I want to do it.'

'Right. Then listen to me. Are you listening?'

'Yes, I'm listening.'

'This is why it has to go . . .'

'Apart from the fact that it's football.'

'Yes. Monday is now the third day of the football weekend, right?'

'Right.'

'Nobody else has a three-day weekend, do they?'

'No, I suppose . . .'

'No other industry. Except on Bank Holidays. And why not?'

'Because . . .'

'It was a rhetorical question. Because it's too much of a good thing. You've only got to look at the average Bank Holiday to know that.'

'Oh, I hate Bank Holidays!'

I knew Ali hated Bank Holidays. He used to say, 'They

are the curse of the self-employed; everybody who should be at work is suddenly on our patch.'

'They're the curse of the self-employed, Ronni; everybody who should be at work is on our patch.'

'I know, Ali. Exactly. Bank Holidays are a curse.'

'They're full of parents dragging children around funfairs,' he says, 'which are never fun and rarely fair. And couples going to buy sofas, smiling forced little smiles as they sit on endless leatherette corner units thinking that leather sofas are still, basically, cold, uncomfortable and too expensive – even with £999 off.'

'Yes, there is that but . . .'

'And they're full of people drinking for the fourth day on the trot, and everyone thinks that everyone else is having a better time . . .'

'Yes, there is that but . . .'

'Parents-in-law come and stay. The roads are all blocked, there's air strikes in France – they're just ghastly!'

'But basically . . .'

'DIY . . . gardening . . . kids on bikes looking lost . . . adults on bikes looking uncomfortable, regattas and castles, someone sitting in for Wogan, *Only Fools and Horses* back-to-back on G.O.L.D. . . . I should think going back to work is normally a pleasant prospect by two in the afternoon for most people . . .'

'Yes. But the basic reason why they're rubbish, Ali, is because they're too much of a good thing. Doing nice things on a Saturday and a Sunday, that's normal. But on a Monday as well? It's too much. It all turns bad – like strawberries in August . . .'

'Or Gary Glitter.'

'Yeah . . . if you like. And Monday-night football.

Monday-night football is too much like that Bank Holiday. The world doesn't need it; you don't need it!'

'Okay, it's gone!'

'Really?'

'Yes.'

My magical powers of persuasion had worked surprisingly quickly again.

'Are you sure you don't want a hot Ribena?'

'No thanks, Ali.'

'Lemon Barley?'

'Haven't you got any coffee, like normal people?'

'No.'

'Well, can you get some for next time?'

'Yes.'

'No one doesn't have coffee.'

'I'll get some.'

'And make sure it's Fair Trade.'

'Yes, Ronni.'

'And stop cleaning the surfaces; there are no crumbs left!'

If you have similar success with the man in your life, I strongly suggest that you replace Monday-night football with something else. Going to the pub together is not enough. Pubs are dangerous: they have screens and show the Monday match. Some restaurants too, especially Italian ones, pander to the whim of their male customers (and their male waiters) and show the Monday match. Gyms and sports clubs have wallpaper television and show the Monday match. A darkened room is best. So I suggest that you make Monday night cinema or theatre night.

To soften the blow, make it seem like football in as many

ways as you can. Have your own post-film or post-show post-match analysis afterwards. Mark the actors out of ten. Discuss who acted well and who performed below their usual standards and should have been taken off. Make sure the performance doesn't just end when the curtain comes down or when the popcorn is all over the floor; show him that every play, every musical, every film is part of a wider picture, a history, a tradition – just like football (but more memorable and without the ugly faces of the men behind the goal – unless Gérard Depardieu is in it).

Ali loves theatre and musicals and films, so I don't have to try too hard to tempt him there; I just need to get him to go more often – especially on Monday nights when *Cabaret* is over.

'How much longer are you in *Cabaret*?'

'Till September.'

'That's months!'

'I know! I love it! It's the best show I've ever been in!'

'Apart from ours.'

'The most fun I've had in anything.'

'Apart from with me?'

'Well . . .'

'Ali!'

'Apart from with you, Ronni.'

But Ali will need other things to fill the next void I am going to create. He doesn't work on Sundays. Sundays are 'Super Sundays', as far as he's concerned. He, and others like him, can now, thanks to Sky, watch three live games on a Super Sunday. They will be next to go.

On a sudden impulse, I hear myself say, 'And, if we're talking Sky, we might as well cut out Super Sundays as well.'

'What?'

'It's a whole day of football – no one needs that. Oh, and that stupid thing on a Saturday afternoon when you watch the TV to watch all those men watching matches on TV. It's ludicrous!'

'I thought we were going to do this gradually!'

'This is gradual.'

'But . . .'

'No arguments, Ali. Just do it!'

'But that's a whole . . .'

'Oh, and I brought you these DVDs. You'll have time now to catch up on a few classics.'

I reach down to my wicker bag and take them out. '*All About Eve*, *Doctor Zhivago*, *Lawrence of Arabia*, *A Night to Remember* and the collected films of Eric Rohmer.'

'Who?'

'They're full of French people looking for love and meaning and . . . bread. You'll love them.'

Ali is stunned and speechless. This feels good!

'And next time, I'll bring you *Trainspotting*.'

'*Trainspotting*?'

'With Ewan McGregor.'

'Me and . . .'

'Leave it!'

I wasn't expecting to do, effectively, three stages in one! This was all going swimmingly. As I go, I can't resist pushing all the neat piles of paper from Ali's desk onto the floor.

'What did you do that for?' Ali asks, indignantly.

'Now you can tidy it up. I just wanted to give you something to look forward to! Bye!'

14

In Bruges

I wait outside the Odeon South Kensington for Ronni. We're going to see *In Bruges*; at least, I presume it's *In Bruges*. I checked the films that are on here when I arrived and couldn't find a film called *About Brussels*. So I presume she meant *In Bruges*. Ronni is late. She's always late. Later than me. I've spent hours of my life waiting for Ronni. But I'm almost as bad.

I've always had a problem with lateness. When I was at drama school, I worked out that if I left Balham Tube station at 8.25, I would arrive at Moorgate at 8.55 and then, with the five-minute walk to the Guildhall School of Music and Drama, I would arrive on the dot of 9 for my first class of the day. But I was always struggling to get to Balham for 8.25. It often meant wrapping up my toast and Marmite to eat out of cling film in front of a bunch of horrified commuters on the Tube.

And it was always because . . . I wanted five more minutes in bed.

What is it about those extra five minutes? Do they really make such a difference? Well, yes, they do. That's why someone invented the 'snooze' button. The wonderful, evil 'snooze' button – the ultimate enemy of the habitually late.

One morning, on the crowded 8.25 Northern Line northbound from Balham, a posh late-runner dragged himself onto the already billowing train by grabbing the rail above our heads and levering himself in. People gasped for breath and room like hungry fish in a bowl.

As the doors shut, pressing us all even closer together, one of the faces of Balham – one of those people that everyone has seen around an area but never heard speak – a tall boy with mean eyes, a mullet and a worn leather jacket with Harley Davidson badges all over it, turned his head as much as he could (about an inch) towards the new arrival and said, in a surprising Scouse accent:

'Well, I bet you think you're really clever, don't you?'

'I'm sorry?'

'Squeezing in and making us all even more uncomfortable.'

'Well, I simply *had* to get on this train!'

'Oh, did you?'

'Yes! I'm sorry but I really am most awfully late!'

And then, the immortal line, in that slow Scouse drawl . . .

'Well, you should have got up earlier then, shouldn't you?'

There was no response. There could be no response.

In that one sentence, The Hairy Scouser summed up the life of everyone who is habitually late. It normally stems from those extra five minutes spent in bed – and we know it. We should have got up earlier, shouldn't we?

To this day, when I'm cursing trains for not running faster, swearing at cars for going too slowly and lights for not changing, and Italians for dawdling and looking at maps, and fat people for just being fat and slow, I always remember the Hairy Scouser's biblical words, 'Well, you should have got up earlier then, shouldn't you?'

I would never say this to Ronni, however. As the mother of two small children she is always up early – and still manages to be late for everything, every time.

At last she arrives, shaking her head and cursing Italians

for dawdling and looking at maps. We happily bypass the sickly E-number heaven/hell of the pick'n'mix and head in to Screen 3, *In Bruges*.

The film is fabulous!

On the way out, Ronni asks me, 'So, marks out of ten?'

'Ten!'

'Man of the match?'

'It's hard to pick one; it was a real team effort. Colin Farrell was superb, though.'

'He always is.'

'Is he? I haven't seen any of his other films.'

'*Phone Booth*?'

'Haven't you got your mobile?'

'It's a Colin Farrell film, Ali.'

'Oh!'

'You see what you've been missing with all your football?'

'I've started the DVDs.'

'Which ones have you seen?'

'*All About Eve*. Tremendous. And some of the French ones. By the way, did you bring *Trainspotting*?'

'Oh, no. I forgot. Next time.'

'We should do this again . . .'

I look into her pretty eyes.

She looks into mine.

'Like old times . . .'

'Yes, like old times.'

'. . . before silly football got in the way.'

'It wasn't just football, Ronni.'

'Let's not row.'

'Shall we go for a coffee? Or something?'

'I've got to get back to the children. God, is that the time?'

And she was gone.

15

Comedy in Tatters

RONNI: I first met Alistair McGowan on a boat on the Thames. Perhaps appropriately, it was a boat that didn't go anywhere. In fact, it was an old paddle-steamer which was acting as 'London's only floating comedy venue'.

Although some of the other comics' backstage drug habits might have made a few of the other venues float for them, this was the only official venue on water. It was easy to see why the idea didn't catch on.

It's still there. And still, I think, a comedy venue. Back then, 'Comedy in Tatters' was the name of the club – a clever pun based on the name of the boat itself, *The Tattershall Castle*. Actually, it's not that clever at all, is it?

But that's where Alistair and I met – one cold Sunday night. Everything was against the little gig really. It was held on a Sunday night, on a boat that was hard to find – and I was frequently the compère . . . well, I shared the compèring with a friend who also organised the night.

I was doing some pretty strange jokes at the time, like, 'I built a wall with my own bare . . . Well, with my own bear.'

Ali told me later that that was actually his favourite of all the jokes I ever did. At the time, he was also wowed by my Diane Keaton impression and the bandanna I used to wear around my wild hair, which my father later poetically described to Alistair as my 'dishcloth round the head' look.

I was so bad that if I had been trendier, I could have been

brilliant – in an ironic, post-modernist, cultish sort of way.

To make matters worse, the audience was normally full of foreign tourists (who didn't realise what was happening and only paid to come on board because they thought the boat did night excursions down the Thames) or people who were in a bad mood because they hadn't got into the 'Improv Night' at the Comedy Store which was the hot Sunday ticket then (and still is!), featuring big stars from *Whose Line Is It Anyway?* like Paul Merton, Josie Lawrence and Mike McShane. Those that couldn't get into the Store were told there was another Comedy Night close by – well, half a mile away, on a hard-to-find boat with a crappy name, poor heating, a silver slash curtain to make it look slightly showbizzy and a compère with a penchant for bad 'bear' jokes.

We did, however, have the most stupendous acts on our bills: Jack Dee, Frank Skinner, Lee Evans, Mark Lamarr and Eddie Izzard all played there. And so did Alistair McGowan . . .

ALISTAIR: I first met Ronni Ancona at a comedy club in Balham – the Balham Banana, at The Bedford pub. It was one of London's best Comedy Nights. The back room where the Comedy Night took place had a lovely domed ceiling and high, arched windows. Trains would flash past on their way to Brighton and the south-east, sending dodgem-car flashes of electric blue around the room every ten minutes. I was the closing act, and Ronni was doing a short unpaid spot in the middle.

I was a little nervous; I was always a little nervous. I stood at the side of the room, watching the two acts before me and casting occasional glances at the audience to see what jokes they were enjoying, who they were. They all seemed to be about twenty-three; they always do. I noticed one very attractive, raven-haired girl in particular who was hovering near the side of the stage, in a red jumper with a strange cloth around her head.

And then, before I went on, she was being introduced onto the stage and was walking up to the microphone: this sweet, lost-looking, tousled-haired creature (in a pair of black jeans and a red, round-necked, baggy jumper) with the most beautiful clavicles I had ever seen. She looked terrified but she went well. She had an odd voice (high and vaguely American), some good material and a weirdness that was quite unique – as if she was surprised by her own ability to be funny, as if she was surprised by everything.

Within minutes of her coming off, I found myself saying, 'Well done, you were great!' She smiled at me from under her blacker than black fringe and thanked me shyly, like a foal that had suddenly discovered the power of speech, but, as I was about to go on, we didn't say much else.

As I was happily seeing somebody else at the time, I didn't think of pursuing anything, but I did find myself hoping that we'd be on a bill together again soon . . .

RONNI: I thought I met you on the boat . . .?
ALISTAIR: That was the second time.
RONNI: Really?
ALISTAIR: Yes. I first saw you in Balham.
RONNI: I don't remember that.
ALISTAIR: In your red jumper.
RONNI: I always wore that jumper; that was my performing jumper.
ALISTAIR: You must remember . . .?

RONNI: I thought that was later?

ALISTAIR: No.

RONNI: Well, after our first meeting on the boat . . .

ALISTAIR: Our second meeting.

RONNI: Yes, but our first meeting *on the boat*.

ALISTAIR: True.

RONNI: I rang Alistair to book him in for another night 'In Tatters' a few months later. My friend was away travelling and had asked me to ring a few comics to make sure the little boat gig carried on in his absence.

ALISTAIR: I thought this was very organised and helpful, and now, being single again, thought how wonderful it would be to have such an organised and helpful girlfriend to do similar things for me.

RONNI: But I'm not really like that.

ALISTAIR: I found that out very quickly.

RONNI: Anyway, I rang Ali . . .

ALISTAIR: And you asked me out.

RONNI: I didn't ask you out.

ALISTAIR: Yes, you did.

RONNI: You asked me . . .

ALISTAIR: I didn't; I was far too shy. And I thought you were still with your 'ex'.

RONNI: No, you asked me. You asked me if I wanted to go and see a film some time.

ALISTAIR: You asked me; if I wanted to see *Shadows and Fogs*, as you called it.

RONNI: It wasn't *Shadows and Fog*, it was *Husbands and Wifes* . . .

ALISTAIR: *Wives*.

RONNI: *Wives*.

ALISTAIR: And you turned up in your red sweater.

RONNI: I wore a white polo neck.

ALISTAIR: And that bashed-up flying jacket.

RONNI: I wore a cream mac. And you wore a white shirt.

ALISTAIR: Black jumper.

RONNI: And your lovely suede jacket.

ALISTAIR: And my lovely suede jacket.

On our first date, there was no indication that Ali had a problem with football – quite the contrary. He seemed artistic, sensitive and romantic. We went, one Friday night in October 1992, to the Screen on the Green in Islington to see Woody Allen's *Husbands and Wifes*.

After the film, we ate chips on a bench in Highbury Fields. We saw each other again the next night. And we fell in love. A week later, after spending a Friday night in North London with me and my two doctor housemates, Peter and Guy (neither of whom even knew what to do with a football), Ali suggested we go to see Spurs play Aston Villa that afternoon. The ground was only 'down the road' from our house in Turnpike Lane, he told us. That was the first time I realised that I was going to have to share him . . .

16

The Belly of the Beast

It had now been twenty days since Ronni had issued her challenge. I knew this was going to get harder but, for the moment, I wasn't missing the football she'd banned me from seeing. It definitely helped that I was working in a West End show at night (when that football was on) and that I was surrounded by gay men (who didn't talk about football) and some scantily clad beautiful young women (who stopped me thinking about football).

But, even so, I was starting to perversely relish the idea of going further with her 'Twelve-Step Programme' and was confident that I could go all the way and give up football bit by bit – and, indeed, live without it for a year, at least. It was starting to become a challenge – and I love a challenge as much as anything.

But there were aspects of giving it up that I knew would be utterly dreadful.

Although I was watching a fraction of my usual football output, I was still in touch with the game. I was reading the results of all the games in the English and Scottish leagues. In fact, I was reading them more than ever, absorbing them like a smoker having a last fag before getting on a long-haul flight. I breathed them in and breathed them deep. Rochdale still looked like they might make the play-offs which were now approaching; there were only a few weeks until the end of the season – and Euro 2008.

England hadn't qualified for the tournament but there

was still publicity for it everywhere: outside pubs, inside pubs, on the newspapers, in the newsagents. Had I been fourteen, I would have been already collecting stickers of players I'd never heard of whose names I couldn't pronounce, sticking them precisely in an album and spending all my late-spring playtimes taking a wad of stickers from my bulging blazer pocket and standing in intimate groups on the school field saying 'Got him, got him, got him . . . haven't got him. Got him, got him, haven't got him' over and over and over again.

Back then, on the school field, I'd always wanted to know more about the game, the players, the gossip, the lives of footballers than I could glean from the occasional newspaper article or magazine. How did it feel to be adored, idolised, hated? Was it terrifying to run out at 3 o'clock on a Saturday? Did you hear the crowd? Did you read the match reports, the transfer gossip, the vitriol? What was it like to have worked with great characters in the game? What went on behind the changing-room door, in the corridors of power, through the doors marked 'Private'?

So I soaked up autobiographies and football books as a child, although they were fairly few and far between and were often no more than dusty-smelling accounts of a pounds-shillings-and-pence era that meant nothing to me. Big shorts, big boots and small change.

In the early 1990s, with my passion for the game totally rekindled after 'the wilderness years' at Leeds University, my mother bought me Lee Chapman's autobiography. Leeds had just won the First Division title, and Lee Chapman had been their leading goalscorer that season (1991–92).

I lapped up Lee's well-written, informative and often very

moving book. It was the furthest I'd seen into the game. But that was about to change.

One afternoon, on Sybil Roscoe's show on Radio 5 Live, I found myself being interviewed alongside former Leeds United footballer Lee Chapman. As shy as I was, I managed after the broadcast to let Lee know that we were neighbours in London SW12. He gave me his card and said that if I ever wanted to go and see him play, I was to call him and he'd sort me out with tickets to see Ipswich – the latest of his many clubs.

After a couple of days of nervous and perfunctorily polite waiting, I rang Lee – shaking like a love-struck teenager. He asked me round to his house and proceeded to show me his England 'B' and Under-21 caps, the match balls he'd been allowed to keep (according to tradition) after scoring hat-tricks (I didn't know they actually did that!), and placed in my hand his League Champions medal – the medal that he'd won with Leeds United! It was like holding the Holy Grail. On top of all that, he gave me, as promised, a ticket for the Ipswich–Aston Villa match the following day. Free! He asked me how I'd get to Ipswich and, unimpressed by my proud statement that I'd take the train, he told me he'd pick me up at 12.30.

I've never been impressed by cars. The whole car culture has always left me cold. Lee Chapman's car, however, was a bit different. It was long, low and dark. I don't know what make it was (you could tell me there was a make of car called 'Cup Cake' and I'd believe you), but the seats were of the finest, softest, whitest leather. It was like being carried along on a cloud. We floated to Ipswich.

All the way there, I asked Lee as casually as was possible – and it's easy to be fairly casual when you're sitting, almost prostrate, on a cumulonimbus – all the questions I'd ever wanted to ask a footballer. Lee, who was as erudite as he was kind, told me everything I could ever have wanted to know.

He'd told me to meet him in the players' lounge after the match (a 0–0 draw in which Lee had only played the last ten minutes as a substitute). The players came through one by one. I'd never been so close to post-performance athletes. Some of them still steamed like horses after a race. This was access beyond my wildest dreams, and no policemen, no barriers, no stewards separated us.

After a brief word here and there, we headed home and all went well until Lee asked me about my 'improvisations', which made me think that either he had misused the word 'impersonations' or thought I was someone else. I changed the subject back to the safety of Leeds United and we floated back into the West End, where I jumped out, ready to hit the Comedy Store again with more football-related stand-up.

I didn't know it as I raced to the Comedy Store but, looking back now, maybe it was the beginning of the end of the affair. I'd crossed the line and a little of the mysticism had gone. Now I knew what lay behind the doors marked 'Private'; I'd seen inside the belly of the beast.

17

A Man's World

Step Six/Seven: Get Him to Give Up Going to Games

I'd actually reached step seven on my list, but as I'd cleverly combined two steps in one last time, I suppose this was the sixth step Ali would be taking. I couldn't find my list anyway and couldn't remember saving it on the computer, so I was improvising again. Six? Seven? Ali wouldn't know. To him, it was just more pain. The self-help books wouldn't have approved, I'm sure. I hadn't had any chance to read them, but they still looked very neat and full of hope on my shelf – a shelf bulging with books that I'll get round to reading one day. But when you have children, you know . . .

Children are welcomed in so many more places these days than they used to be. But there is nothing particularly child-friendly about the football match – certainly not the live football match. As the song says, 'It's a man's world,' and that's probably more true of the football ground than anywhere else.

That Spurs game I went to with Ali, on our second date, was my first trip to a football match. I'll always remember the approach to the ground, to this other world: the noise of men's feet on the hard roads on their unshaven day off; the rustle of men's clothes – the big leather jackets that smelt of pubs and porches and bacon and beer and old hair and arms; the vans selling grey meat, half hot, covered in soggy onions, the coagulated sauce bottles; the unsold badges for sale on black nylon-covered boards; fathers and sons; policemen on horses trying to look friendly; the clack of the hooves; the distant chants, the threats; the chatter and the buzz I didn't understand.

Then, once I was through those cold, steel turnstile things, the very smell of football – cold concrete and wet grass, old mustard and frothy urine – hit me full in the face. There would be how many minutes of this? Ninety! An hour and a half. With an interval. Or half-time. Or whatever it was called. That was almost two hours of my life! I thought of all the other things I could be doing – and then looked at Ali's lop-sided smiling face, at his lovely suede jacket that I had already started to love a bit, and told myself to enjoy it – for his sake.

And suddenly, dear Ali was talking to me. Trying to make it more interesting for me. Talking about the teams, the players. Who played where. Who'd played for England. And Scotland. And France. And Trinidad and Tobago! I was hit by the volume of the tannoy – the self-important announcements about birthdays and badly parked cars and the next match (did they think I was coming back?!) – and the mounting tension I sensed but knew I would never really feel.

And out they came, these heroes. Everyone was on their feet. I stood and clapped too, and wondered why. Clapped these twenty-two men for being there. Because I was there. Because Ali did. He clapped along and, smiling at each other, we added to the sound of thousands of gloved hands, all trying to make more noise than they could.

What do they do to deserve this, I wondered, these play-ers? And why is Ali doing this? Does he really worship these men? These boys? It was a man's world. It was my man's world. It ended 0–0.

I find my list; it was in the fridge under a yoghurt.

(1) Find the root cause of the addiction to football ✓
(2) Give up Match off the Day
(3) Give up the Champions League ✓
(4) Get him interested in other sports ✓
(5) No more Monday-night football ✓
(6) No more not-so-Super Sundays ✓
(7) No more going to football games
(8) No more reading about it all in the papers
(9) No more watching England games – esp. 'friendlies'
(10) Take him to cultural events

I call Ali. It was time for him to give up going to the game.

18

Terraced Cottages

'I just can't see why you want to do it, why anyone would want to do it.'

'You saw one game, Ronni!'

'Two games!'

'Okay, two games! I could see two films that didn't excite me but that wouldn't mean I wouldn't go to the cinema ever again. And think of all the different sorts of films there are. Similarly, there's lots of different sorts of football matches.'

'What? Are there sci-fi football matches? And weepy football matches? And Westerns? Do all the players dress up as cowboys sometimes? That I would like to see . . .'

Ronni has asked me to go for a walk. For once, I agreed. But there was a purpose to it. I'm having my ceiling replaced after my upstairs neighbour let her shower flood my bathroom again, and Ronni is trying to shed baby weight. So it's not just a pointless stroll leading to an overpriced antique shop. She said she wanted 'a little chat' as well and that she'd come to me.

So we find ourselves wandering by the River Thames between Hammersmith and Putney, approaching the beautiful facade of Fulham Football Club (the quaintly named Craven Cottage) on a sunny morning in May. Our little chat is in danger of developing into a row.

'Live games don't affect you, anyway. They're not in your house. Under your feet. They're in grounds like . . .'

'If you're going to give up football, Ali, surely you have to give up the live experience.'

'But if it's away from the house and away from you . . . I mean, look at this lovely ground, Ronni. It still excites me even though it's totally empty.'

'Oh, God! That's like . . . sniffing a fag packet!'

'Look, the football ground is the heart of the community. Look at this place. Right next to all these terraced houses. By the river. There used to be a little ferry boat at the back that brought people over the river from Barnes. It's called Fulham and it's in Fulham for the people of Fulham. And Barnes, obviously.'

'Oh, come on! Look at these houses. All ceiling lights and polished floors and corner cupboards. I bet they hate match day. I don't think they *live* for Fulham Football Club.'

'There's a Fulham scarf in that window! And another! Think how excited those little boys must be. This is their club. On their doorstep! They can walk down the road and see them play.'

'For forty quid a pop. Kids haven't got that sort of money.'

'It's not that much.'

'It is at Chelsea.'

'This isn't Chelsea.'

'It's twenty-five at Millwall, and they're in League One.'

'How do you know that?'

'I checked.'

'You're really getting into football, aren't you?'

'No! I'm getting into getting you out of football. And live matches are out of the price range of most of the people they used to attract. Doesn't that just seem wrong to you?'

'They still go.'

'Exactly. They still go. That's what the clubs know. "They

will still come, so we can charge them all this money for a ticket. And they're suckers for 'things', so let's offer them programmes at £5 a throw too. And overpriced kits and comb cases and ladies pants with club motifs and junk food, and then throw away all the money they give us on a bunch of overhyped foreign players who only chose to play for this team anyway because we offered them the most money!"'

'That's not true!'

'It's no longer a part of the community, Ali. The ground just happens to be here. The players have next to no connection with the area. They're not two teams of local players; they're two corporations playing each other.'

'Half my old Leeds team was from Scotland. Billy Bremner, Eddie Gray, Peter Lorimer. They were all Scots, Ronni. So were . . .'

'Yes, but they were from Scotland, not Paraguay! These fans would probably happily go on demos wanting "British jobs for British workers", but they don't care who plays for their football team – as long as their team wins!'

'But that shows a spirit of . . .'

'No! It's total hypocrisy and you know it, Ali.'

God, she's hard to argue with.

I'd always wanted to live near a football ground, to feel part of the football community. After 'the change', I went to Coventry for a few games with a friend of mine called David Pettifer. David's family had come from Coventry and, though he now lived near Evesham, his nan still lived in the city.

Once or twice, we set off early and stopped off to see David's nan. She lived near the ground (Highfield Road), and as kick-off approached we'd see and hear the fans walking and talking to the match. The chatter of friends, the footsteps of Saturday shoes, the sound of freedom, the Talbot and Singer factory workers walking into the free fresh air of a day at the match. And, across the sauce bottles and the permanently tableclothed table, I could feel the excitement outside David's nan's window. This is what football should be, what it was: community.

'But, Ronni,' I say, daring to argue again in the hope that (as she always rather charmingly puts it) her train of thought will fall into her stream of consciousness, 'going to the match is still part of the weekend for many men: finish work on Friday, out on the town on Friday night, fish and chips at lunchtime on Saturday and a football match on Saturday afternoon. It's where they vent their anger. It's where . . .'

'What anger?'

'Their anger at everything. Being unable to shout at their boss, they shout at the ref; unable to shout at their workmates, they shout at their own players; unable to shout at their wives, they shout at the opposition fans. It's an outlet! And they belong! They own the club!'

'No, no, no, Ali! Listen to me! Are you listening to me?'

I nod and sigh. And listen.

'The club owns *them*, Ali, just like cigarettes own smokers and drugs own a junkie. It's not their *choice*. They think they're in control, but they're not!'

'No one forces you to go to football.'

'Peer groups do, surely, once it becomes a habit.'

'As habits go, it's a great habit. And anyway . . .'

'Look, Ali, I can understand people wanting to follow their team. The tribal, primal aspect of it all, being part of "a community"'.

Ronni did the quotation marks with her fingers in that annoyingly patronising way that people do.

'. . . all that . . .'

'But . . .?'

'But . . . why let that take over your life outside the match?'

'Because if you belong, you belong! City till you die, Fulham till you die, football till you die.'

'But most football fans deny themselves so many other experiences by just living for ninety minutes a week!'

'It's tradition; it's . . . family!'

'I can totally appreciate that. I mean, who wouldn't be stirred by the sight of generations of fans cheering for the team their father and grandfather supported?'

'You!'

'No. Even me, Ali, even me. But the tragedy is, the game they're cheering about is so fundamentally dull!'

'It's not always about the game.'

'What?'

'I said, "It's not always about the game"!'

'Well, what else is there? Police-dog display teams? Tell me they don't come to see that! "Oh, yeah, I put up with ninety minutes of overpriced tedium so that I get to see the police-dog display team at half-time" . . .'

'They don't do that sort of thing any more. Anyway, most fans, Ronni,' I say, trying very hard to keep my patience, 'most fans will tell you that the game is secondary. It's about a day out. The bonding. The privacy of being in a crowd.'

'Oh, spare me the martyrdom! And the oxymoron.'

'The collective orgasm of a goal.'

'And certainly spare me the homoerotica!'

'Listen, you just don't get it, Ronni, and you never will!!!!'

'Stop shouting, Ali!'

'I'm not shouting!!!'

'You are! That man's looking at you.'

I am shouting. I take a breath. I'm riled.

'Going to a game is the most pure thing. It's like distilled football.'

'Oh, pur-leaze!'

'Ronni, listen!'

'Don't tell me to listen! Have you any idea how patronising that is?'

I take an even deeper breath. 'I can understand you not enjoying going to games, so don't go. But let those people who do want to go, go and enjoy themselves!'

'You can't give up football, Ali, if you're still going to live games. That's like . . .'

She paused.

'Like what?'

'I don't know. I can't think of an analogy right now but anyway it's on my programme. Step eight. Six. "No more live games."'

'Bloody hell! Bloody, bloody pissing hell!'

'Keep your voice down!'

In my experience, women could put men off going to matches fairly easily by simply going to the matches with them. Especially by asking them embarrassing questions which are audible to the surrounding fans. This has happened to me on a couple of occasions. When Ronni and I went to our game together at Spurs, I remember her saying, quite audibly as the team mascots ran out, 'Who are the ones in the furry suits? Are they the players who didn't get picked?' It got a great laugh from those around us, until they realised she was serious. They heard me explaining the inherent impracticality of her idea. Then they turned round and nodded with admiration and sympathy.

On another occasion (at Nottingham Forest), I was asked by the girl I'd gone with to explain the offside rule there and then. After I'd finally made the rule understandable to her, I remember, the two men in front of me turned round and nodded with admiration and sympathy.

And the very first time I ever took a girlfriend to the match, she had begun shouting 'Come on!' to all the wrong players, despite the fact that I kept saying Coventry were in sky blue. The fans thought we were both in the wrong end and turned round threateningly. Then they saw my colours and my predicament, and nodded with admiration and sympathy.

Ronni and I walked towards the River Café, and the fresh semi-seaside smell of the low tide calmed me down a little.

'Do you know, I once knew a Birmingham City fan who wouldn't let his girlfriend wear claret or blue because they're Aston Villa's colours.'

'Well, he was doing her a favour, then; they look terrible together.'

'When he goes on holiday, he won't even stay "in a villa".'

'That's ridiculous!'

'I know. You can take these things too far.'

'Says the man who wouldn't eat in an Argentinian restaurant.'

'What?'

'Don't you remember that time, Ali, when my friend Jenny was staying with us . . .'

'Oh, lovely Jenny!'

'Yes, all right, I know you always fancied her.'

'I only said . . .'

'And remember we went out to eat? And we walked all the way down Northcote Road in Clapham and all the restaurants were full, except for an Argentinian one. And you refused to go in . . .'

'Oh, yes, well, that . . .'

'"Why?" we said. "Why, Ali? Surely not because of the Falklands?" "No," you said, "because of Maradona's Hand of Gold."'

'Hand of God.'

'I mean, come on! You're an intelligent man!'

'Well, I don't feel like that now. I ate in an Argentinian restaurant last year in Alicante – it was very nice food.'

'Yeah, I know, but you said you only agreed to eat there because David Beckham had scored against Argentina from a dodgy penalty in the World Cup to knock them out in the quarter-final . . .'

'Round before the quarter-final.'

'In, erm . . .'

'2002 in Japan.'

'"Honours even," you said.'

'Well . . .'

'Anyway, live games have got to go, Ali.'

I knew this would be hard. I'd always loved going to games, even if my team (whoever they were at the time) weren't playing. The first sight of the impossibly lush grass, the sound of the tannoy, the buzz and the growing chatter among friends, that feeling of, 'I'm in! This'll be on telly later, the result will be on the radio, in the papers. I'll be in the attendance figure – without me there would have been one less.'

I still get excited by all that but I guess she's right. If I'm giving it all up, I'm giving it all up.

We nip into the River Café to use the toilets.

'Wait for me here,' says Ronni, pointing animatedly at a spot just between the two toilet doors.

She always says this. I never understand it. Where else would you wait? Maybe she's worried about losing me. Or has read stories in women's magazines about countless relationships foundering when women went into the Ladies toilets at the same time as their partners went into the Gents, only to return to find them gone for ever. 'I Went to the Toilet and Lost Him For Ever!'

That's what you read when you don't read about football, I suppose.

We meet at her pointedly pointed-to appointed place.

'You will come and see *Cabaret*, won't you, Ronni?'

'I'm coming.'

'Well, come soon because there are rumours we're closing . . .'

'No! That's awful!'

'Just rumours. There's always rumours.'

'I'll come. I've been very busy. But when you have children . . .'

'I know.'

'I'm sorry we had a row.'

'Me too.'

'But I am right.'

We say goodbye and go our separate ways. I look back to wave at Ronni. She doesn't look back. Ronni never looks back.

Maybe I should learn something from that.

19

Getting Serious

Step Eight: No More Reading About It All in the Papers

A photographer friend of mine once said that he realised he was a grown-up when he started having a newspaper delivered. It was one of those signs. Like going to Debenhams for your jumpers, opening an account at John Lewis or buying underwear for your boyfriend in sets of three.

Sadly, however, you are probably the only one in your relationship reading that newspaper like a grown-up: from front to back – not from back to front – possibly removing the arts section to read over a fruit smoothie.

Because, if your man is a football fan, he will spend most of the morning over breakfast reading nothing but the football news and reports on the back pages. And, if it's a Sunday, he could be reading that extra-long sports section (in all its self-contained glory) for anything up to three hours.

Alistair never reads any section of the Sunday papers other than the sport, and this normally takes him all day; in fact, he can be two hours looking at just the results, fixtures and other useless statistics page.

He is not alone in this.

The front page could lead with 'Moon Explodes' or a story about Australia dropping 20 degrees south, and he wouldn't know. Nor would many men.

In the arts section, Madonna could be trying to adopt Angelina Jolie, and he wouldn't know. Nor would many men. The financial pages could have announced how Fidel Castro had abandoned his political ethos to start his own hedge fund, and Alistair wouldn't know. Mind you, neither would I. Or you. Nobody reads the financial pages. How do I know? Because if anybody other than bankers had read anything about the financial world over the last two years surely we'd have seen that the credit crunch was on the way and likely to wipe trillions off the markets and millions of smiles off millions of faces, and we'd have done something about it! But no, the majority of people, the majority of men, were too busy trying to work out Rochdale's chances of reaching the play-offs to see financial disaster winging its way over from America like a huge black cash-eating bird.

This is the danger of reading about nothing but football.

Alistair is coming round this morning to let me know how he's getting on with his withdrawal programme. It's a Sunday and I'm listening to Radio 4. I realise, however, that it's just about time for *The Archers* omnibus and I can't take any chances – Alistair hates *The Archers* and usually runs screaming from the house if he hears so much as the theme tune. I switch over to Michael Ball on Radio 2. Show tunes; he'll like that. I think not for the first time how football is the one thing that stops Ali being gay. That and his absolute love of women, obviously.

The buzzer sounds and Alistair's face appears like a strange eagle in the fish-eye screen by the door. As I let him in, I tell him, disingenuously, that he has a day off from the programme.

'So make yourself at home while I go and get us the Sunday papers.' (I'm still not grown up enough to have set up a delivery.)

He looks confused but happy, no doubt picturing the page of league tables and goalscorers that will be coming his way. As I leave for the shop, he has already started wiping my surfaces with a cloth.

On the way back from the newsagent's, I remove the sports supplements from the two newspapers and drop them in a recycling bin. Once home, I throw the papers in front of him and pretend to be getting him some orange juice, while I secretly watch him sifting through the sections, at first puzzled he can't find the sports bit in either paper. This develops into fully fledged panic as he realises that his precious pages aren't there. It becomes almost too unbearable to watch. He looks like a trapped animal, his long arms flailing around.

I almost feel sorry for him. He is bereft and wide-eyed, like a drug addict needing his fix. I say I must have dropped them or maybe the man in the shop didn't put them in. I suggest he could look at some other sections first or maybe he could retrace my steps and see if, indeed, I did drop them. If it hadn't been pouring with rain, I'm sure he'd have done it too.

He looks at me, suddenly clearly thinking that to lose one sports section is unfortunate but to lose two sounds like a plot. Only one thing will distract him: toast and Marmite. To avoid any scenes, I have bought a supply. I head to the kitchen. He heads back to the mangled pile of review sections and business pages to continue hunting for what's not there, clawing at the noisy pages like some large, balding kitten.

Three minutes later, my plan seems to have failed. As I bring him his toast, I see that he is happily ensconced in an article alongside a picture of David Beckham hugging Ashley Cole. But it's okay. It's a rogue piece in the travel section . . . about World Cup tickets and trips!

I swear Alistair sniffed that out in a matter of seconds. Ah, the comfort of those familiar images of childhood . . .!

I tell him how desperate he looked, and I can see it hurts him. Not watching the Champions League had been easy. This was a competition, let's not forget, which had no connection with his past, with his childhood, with his father. Live games he hadn't been to for a while. Monday nights he doesn't miss yet because he's surrounded at work every night by women in their pants. Sunday football? Well, we'll see how he's coping without that come 1.30. But reading the results on a Sunday morning goes deeper. Much deeper.

It was time to get Ali to give up the habit of a lifetime. He had to stop reading about football. And not just in the papers – everywhere. Even on Ceefax. I give him a list of banned reading areas. Oh, yes! I'm getting very organised now! I haven't typed it up, but even so, he'll enjoy it – he can pin his list to his bedroom wall and tick them off one by one.

20

Bashing My Manhood

So now she wants me to stop reading about football. Can you believe that? She's even given me a list. It says:

No newspapers.
No magazines.
No Ceefax.
No reports.
No opinion pieces.
Get Calpol.
No transfer gossip.
No interviews with young players about their favourite music.
No stats.
Make ears for crocodile costume.
No league tables!!
Good luck!

Well, it was a list of sorts. And there would be no cutting down slowly with this one. This was only one step in the programme, but it was a mighty one. I've been reading about football ever since I got bored with banging round plastic pegs through round plastic holes with a big plastic hammer. I have a huge knowledge of the game. Its history, its players, its teams, its big matches, its tournament winners – I know it all.

I've been popular in pub quizzes because of my knowledge of football; heck, I've even been on a Christmas edition of *A Question of Sport*! And that sort of knowledge doesn't just happen. It has to be worked at. You have to put the hours in. If you want to hold your own in a changing room, in a pub or at work, with mates who support every club from Arsenal to York City, you have to devote yourself to reading about football.

You want to have that nugget up your sleeve when your old friend takes you to Birmingham City for the first time in ten years: the capacity of the ground, who they bought their centre-forward from, who the manager used to manage, who their leading scorer is this season, who it was last season and with how many goals. That sort of stuff is impressive and takes careful study.

I have always, always, always read about football. Every day of my life. Even in the summer, when the papers are full of cricket and tennis and athletics, I read the tiny football bits twice over to make up for the lack of verbiage. I remember those awful childhood summer days when it wasn't worth looking at my dad's *Daily Express*, when there were no lists of fixtures to look forward to, no results to catch up on or predict; just lists of strange, long cricket statistics that meant nothing to me and the names of Aussie rules football clubs squatting in the place of the regular weekend football fixtures like fat and messy students.

Reading about football was my favourite pastime. This was going to hurt. Really hurt. It was going to be impossible. Wasn't it . . .?

It was one of the many arguments Ronni and I had had about football years ago in our red front room in Clapham.

'Sports results, Ali,' she said one Sunday morning (in fact, every Sunday morning), 'you hear on the radio or see on the telly – or both! – and why do you need to read reports about matches today that you saw last night on *Match of the Day*? Put the sports pages away and read something else, Ali. And then we can talk about something else. About something!'

Initially, being a stubborn sort, I dug in and kept reading the football pages feverishly – every report, every result, every league table, every bit of transfer speculation, every interview with a young player about his favourite music. And then I started to realise that she was right. I started reading her bits over her shoulder. I'd find myself starting to read about whether or not this player or that player might be moving from or staying at Leicester City, who had played well for Manchester City against Norwich the day before, and think, 'Why am I reading this? Why do I need to know this? I could be reading something more important . . . or doing any number of other things.'

So, from then on, reading football reports, at least, had more or less gone from my life.

Then, slowly, 'after Ronni', it had all crept back into my life again. I was the smoker who gave in to 'the odd one' – the odd report, the occasional bit of transfer gossip – and before I knew it, I was back on forty a day. And now I can easily listen to a match on the radio on a Saturday afternoon, watch the highlights of the same match on *Match of the Day* on Saturday evening and then read about that match in the papers on a Sunday morning, watch the highlights of the highlights of that match on *Match of the Day 2* on the Sunday evening and then read about that two-day-old match from a different angle on the Monday.

Why do I do this? There is not going to be a test!

So I could give up the match reports; I'd done it before.

But I couldn't give up the results then. And I couldn't give up the attendances . . .

Ah, the attendances! I've always needed to know the attendance of every game played in the football league. I've always been that way, ever since I knew what the mysterious number under a result meant. I must have been about seven when I finally got to know. In those days, if Leeds lost I was devastated. But I'd think, 'Well, at least maybe Leeds might "get the numbers"'. I didn't know what these numbers meant, but I thought maybe there was some higher game going on whereby if your team 'got the numbers' under them it was some sort of code for points that might be added up at the end of the season, resulting in some bonus – a bit like Green Shield Stamps. It always seemed to be the losing side that 'got the numbers'.

One day, in desperation, I asked my dad what 'the numbers' meant. I prepared myself for a lengthy answer: a lot of football's machinations involved quite lengthy answers and the use of applied maths which, being one for figures, I relished.

'The numbers?' said my dad.

'Yeah . . .'

'It's not "yeah", it's "yes".'

'Yes. The numbers in the paper. Not the score, Dad, but the numbers . . .'

'Show me!'

I pointed to the numbers under the name of Leeds United.

'Oh!' said my dad, chuckling through clouds of acrid pipe smoke. 'That's the attendance.'

'The what?'

'The gate.'

'The what?'

'The number of people in the crowd, son.'

I was disappointed to think that 'the numbers' were not going to magically help Leeds win the league, but then, of course, I became obsessed with attendances. Over the years, they have come to mean to me what the alignment of the planets meant to the Elizabethans. They believed that if the political and social order was maintained, then the planets would remain aligned and everything would be all right with the world. So 'all right', in fact, that the metaphorical harmony of this planetary alignment produced a truly audible harmony which they called 'the music of the spheres'. But, if one thing should change in the political or social order, the alignment of the planets would alter and 'discord' (in every sense) would follow.

This is how I feel about attendances. Attendances now are fairly predictable. You can bank on the fact that there will be about 2,500 people to watch Macclesfield play Darlington, and 38,000 to see Everton play Fulham. So if there were suddenly 25,000 people at Macclesfield v. Darlington, or just 3,800 people at Everton v. Fulham, this to me would signify impending world catastrophe – an audible 'discord' in the music of the spheres. I need to check the attendance of every match to know that if there has been a highly irregular attendance, I will be prepared for it, prepared for the shift in the world order or, at least, prepared for the conversation that will follow. Like everything to do with football stats, you don't want to be the one who doesn't know.

I remember the day a couple of years ago when I hadn't been able to pick up a Sunday paper before meeting my friend Dan, who is almost more obsessed with football stats than I am, and he asked me, had I noticed that two games in League Two had had attendances of 4,444? I hadn't.

'What', he said, 'are the chances of having two attendances exactly the same on one day? And what are the chances then of that attendance being a figure made up of only one digit?'

It was super-symmetry. And highly portentous. Surely, on this basis, an Elizabethan gentleman would have been running from hamlet to hamlet proclaiming that the end of the world was nigh.

'It could, however, be a misprint,' said Dan.

I said, 'We should check on Ceefax.'

'But the attendances aren't kept on Ceefax overnight,' said Dan – something which we both agreed we always found frustrating.

We could have bought another paper to see if 'the mistake' was replicated, but the Newcastle game we were about to watch together at his home (no. 62) was starting and the paper shop was too far away for us to get there and back and check the attendance without missing the beginning.

By the end of the game, Newcastle United's plight had taken over in our thoughts and the evil attendance omen had been carelessly forgotten. But nothing dreadful occurred; perhaps we'd been lucky this time.

Suffice to say, in general, knowing the attendances of all the games played in England and Scotland brings me comfort. And now I have to give all that up?!

Will I be able to survive?

On the first day after the reading ban, I am on the Tube going into the theatre. There are free newspapers everywhere. I would normally pick them up and seek solace, escape and reassurance in the football reports, scores and attendances on the back pages. I can see headlines, but I try not to read them.

I think of what I've been telling myself: it's the same stories every season, just with different names – spitting incidents, suspensions, disallowed goals that should have been, players getting in trouble in the tunnel, managers criticising each other's conduct, a bad tackle, a lengthy injury lay-off, an impending transfer, and articles about whether a certain big club is ever going to regain its former status. Everything is interchangeable. It's only the names that change – except that the big club trying and failing to regain its former glory is always Newcastle United.

This is a sick plot that I have been drawn into. There are so many other things in life, so many other sections of a newspaper, and yet those free newspapers sit there, teasing me with their pictures and stories about transfers and games played and games to come – simple things. Easy things. Football doesn't really matter; that's why I read about it. It's not terminally depressing (unless you're a Southampton fan). Those lovely, cosy, friendly back pages aren't full of stories of cruelty or impending world economic or ecologic disaster.

I pick up a discarded copy and, ignoring temptation, actually start reading it from the front to the back. It feels odd. I'd always read papers from the back page forwards. It's like suddenly trying to butter a piece of bread with my feet, and with very hard, cold butter. There are league tables in here somewhere, but I mustn't look! I try not to look. It's hard. Like not popping bubble wrap. But I resist, sweating slightly.

It feels all wrong! What was this lack of football going to do to me? It was, after all, my last bastion of maleness. My 'manhood' was taking a bashing. Piccadilly Circus. Time to get off the Tube and put on my stockings, leather shorts and basque . . .

What would my father say?

21

My Football Past

It was really quite funny seeing Ali panic without the sports sections last weekend. And it will definitely do him good to read about other things than football; it does genuinely take up so much of his life. It used to drive me mad years ago. All those wasted Sunday mornings; he couldn't do anything until he'd devoured all those football facts and figures. He was an intelligent man; why did he need to know them so well? I could never understand it. There wasn't going to be a test!

But I suppose I can't be too derogatory about this football association of Ali's. I don't mean *the* Football Association, which I can be very derogatory about; I mean the habit that Ali and many fans have of associating nearly everything back to football in order to feel safe and happy or something equally pathetic.

You see, there was a time when football had been immensely useful in my life.

When Ali and I first met, I was a stand-up comic at night but a teacher by day. My life had descended into a perpetual stream of humiliation: I was heckled by night and heckled by day.

The school was Holloway Boys School. Holloway, famous mainly for its prison, sits quietly in the shadow of two of London's biggest football clubs – two of Britain's biggest football clubs. So all the pupils at Holloway were either ardent Arsenal fans or strident Tottenham fans. They lived, breathed and fought for their clubs. Fought each other – in the playground. In the corridors. In my art and design classes. With their feet. With their elbows. With compasses.

There was enough overt aggression going on in that school without the added complication of one of football's biggest rivalries simmering under the surface, waiting to explode. So I hated Arsenal and I hated Tottenham for making my job so unnecessarily difficult.

The boys were not what you might describe as 'boys' – not in the *Peter Pan* sense. There were no spindly legs and National Health glasses at Holloway Boys School, no wooden swords and cardboard shields. My boys were really 'young men' – and big, strong young men at that.

Every lesson I taught would start with total disinterest, build to a sweaty apathy and then dissolve into some sort of general pushing and shoving about who was the better team: Arsenal or Spurs? It was all I ever heard. 'Arsenal or Spurs?' It drove me mad. All this was also when Arsenal were winning a lot of things and Tottenham weren't. So the discussion was pretty irrelevant anyway. Arsenal, at the time, were clearly better. I kept this little piece of logic to myself for fear of upsetting the blue and white half of the room.

The boys were never very interested in my endless, earnest attempts to teach them about composition, shading and perspective. Then, one day, I hit on an idea. I, for my sins, was what was now called an art, design and technology teacher, so when we got onto the design bit (and textiles in particular), I asked them to design a new kit for their favourite football team. The room was suddenly totally quiet. Not in a prissy prep-school wide-eyed silence of 'total quiet' but the sort of 'total quiet' in which I could, at least, almost hear myself speak for once above the perpetual rumble of 'dissing'. Thirty-odd boys got their heads down and drew and designed and dreamt. They began to ask me about the merits of certain fabrics, about colours, about patterns. I'd got them – for the first time in a year!

From then on, I tried to incorporate football into everything I taught them. It wasn't easy to make the Surrealists relevant to Tottenham and Arsenal but I tried. I think I said that the Surrealists and Dadaists were violently opposed to each other and fought in the streets and theatres of Paris, a bit like Arsenal and Tottenham fans do now. It seemed to work.

I used football to teach because it was the *only* way to get through to them. Suddenly, football was my friend, but, on the other hand, if the boys hadn't been so obsessed with it, maybe they would have been more interested in other things from the start. They were potentially very bright boys – completely anaesthetised by football.

Football took up all their thinking time – at the age of fourteen, most of them were already addicts. Some of them, I was told, were very talented players; they may have gone on to make a career of it for all I know. But it was more likely that they'd be left with nothing but shattered dreams and an ignored education. Thanks, Arsenal. Thanks, Spurs. Thanks, football.

22

Arsenal, 1993

I've been cycling into the West End regularly for *Cabaret*. It's about six miles, much of it along cycle lanes. Cycle lanes have definitely improved in London (and, indeed, throughout the country) but they still have a habit of suddenly totally disappearing without any warning. It's as if the whole network has been designed by Derren Brown.

Today, however, it was absolutely tipping it down with rain. So I went in by Tube and am now heading back in a taxi. The driver asks me what I thought of the Cup Final last weekend. I realise that for the first time in my life, I hadn't even known the Cup Final was happening. I tell him about Ronni's plan – about my challenge.

'Bloody hell!' he says. 'I couldn't do that! I live for me football. 'avin' said that, it has ruined my relationships. I love my 'ammers so much. That's why my last two wives left me in the end. Yeah. They said it was West 'am or them. And I chose West 'am, mate. West 'am give me things no woman ever could. I tell you, I watch football all day and all night – from all over the world. I do that Championship Manager too. D'you ever do that?'

'No, I'm hopeless with . . .'

'Oh, it just eats up the hours, like. But I love it. I live for me football, me. I couldn't have another relationship now. And d'you know what? It don't bother me. Me football's more important, like.'

Maybe Ronni was saving me from this. As he continued

to talk about the Cup Final and the Hammers, even though I'd told him I didn't really want to talk football at the moment, my thoughts drifted back to my relationship with Ronni; to the Cup Final we'd been to, to the part football had played in our relationship. I used to tell her it gave us our bread and butter – and jam. But it did come between us. It was our 'Camilla'. From the start, I suppose.

The first time I ever got to entertain footballers in the flesh was in 1993, while Ronni was still teaching at Holloway. I had a phone call from a man called Jonty Atkinson. He was Ian Wright's agent; in fact, he represented, he said, most of the Arsenal team at that time. Arsenal had just performed the unusual feat of winning both the domestic cups – the FA Cup and the Coca-Cola Cup (now the Carling Cup) – in the same season. Ian Wright was their most famous player, loved by Arsenal fans and hated by most other fans because he was a bit arrogant, very cheeky and scored lots of goals against their teams. He was particularly adored by Ronni's pupils at Holloway Boys School. Here, I thought, was possibly a chance to make things up to her, to get football on her side.

I was asked to do 'about twenty minutes of football stuff' at the Park Lane Hotel in Mayfair at a special end-of-season dinner for the double cup-winning players. Twenty minutes! I had only about fifteen minutes of football stuff, and about ten minutes of *good* football stuff. But I wasn't going to say no.

I was to 'speak' after Duncan McKenzie. Duncan McKenzie had played for Leeds United. He was signed by Brian Clough from Nottingham Forest during Clough's famously ill-fated forty-four-day reign as Leeds manager, and had always been, for me, a symbol of the beginning of the end of the real Leeds. The Revie Leeds. But he'd nevertheless rubbed shoulders with my heroes. To hear him speak was an honour. McKenzie had a dry, piping voice and a northern accent, and kept apologising to 'any ladies present' for anything approaching bad language or the slightest of sexual references. He was, as I'm sure he'd admit, an odd choice for Arsenal's double cup-winning celebrations at the Park Lane Hotel in 1993.

I, however, found myself wrapped up in his stories of Bremner and Lorimer and Clarke and Clough. But no one else was really listening. This was, as they say, 'a tough crowd'.

But I'd done the Comedy Store many times by now and knew I could win over most difficult crowds, especially difficult male crowds – they always loved my football stuff.

So after Duncan McKenzie had finished his speech, I stood up at top table, looked out at the two round tables of famous England internationals who then played for Arsenal, swallowed, took a deep breath and launched into my failsafe opening gag.

'Imagine Gary Lineker on his wedding night. After the big event, I bet his wife turns to him and says, "How was it for you, Gary?" And Gary says, "Well, obviously it's the sort of thing every young lad dreams about, Michelle, but, at the end of the day, it's just about being in the right place at the right time really – and attacking the space!"'

It got next to nothing. I stared at them; they stared at me.

I moved swiftly on to some specially written Arsenal gags. You often get an easier laugh at material which has clearly been written for one specific night. The audience feels spoilt. They'll excuse the odd flaw because you've made an effort and done something just for them.

Not this night. The Arsenal squad sat before me, in the centre of the Ballroom, staring at me, unmoved.

I made a joke about their centre-forward, Alan Smith, having 'a nose for goal' ('Smudger' was, like me, well-endowed in the nasal area), at which he, and most of the players . . . just frowned.

I told better, more well-worn jokes about other teams' players' haircuts, about crowd chants, did impressions of Victor Meldrew as Trevor Brooking ('as for John Motson, he wouldn't know a sharp bloody angle if you poked him in the eye with one'), of Alan Hansen telling his children the Nativity story ('The angel of the Lord comes down, we've circled him here . . .'), of Brian Clough ('Good managers are like good wine – not that they mature with age, no. They get drunk very quickly'). Even Graham Taylor singing a Beatles song – a joke Harry Hill helped me write, for God's sake! – got nothing. It was at least 1–0 to The Arsenal.

The silence seemed to go on for ever. I paused. My mind had stopped working. Should I just quit now? Sit down and pretend it hadn't happened? My mouth was impossibly dry. My impressions were starting to waver; I couldn't get my tongue or my lips into the right places – everything was too dry. My brain was tired. I'd been working on this all day and now their lack of response was giving me no thinking time in-between the 'gags'. I'd only done about six minutes of football stuff; the rest was newly written and unreliable.

I fell back on my usual Comedy Store set, featuring the voices of Rolf Harris and Moira Stuart, Antoine de Caunes and Ian McCaskill. Would the players even know who these people were? Of course they would! They watched telly too, didn't they? Apparently not. Irony, wordplay, surreality, innuendo – nothing seemed to get them.

Arsenal were famous for having a strong defence – well, I certainly couldn't get past them that night. The defence or the midfield. They sat and blinked slowly, repelling my every foray into their funny bones. The manager, the sober and dour George Graham, looked at me soberly and dourly for twenty minutes. David Seaman, the man well known for having the biggest smile and the loudest laugh in football, didn't smile and didn't laugh.

And then I noticed: one man among them was visibly laughing at anything. One man was audibly laughing – at everything. One Arsenal player stood at the end and clapped and cheered. That man was Ian Wright.

To compose myself (and because I couldn't face sitting down next to the man who'd booked me and watch him trying to pretend it had gone well) I went straight to the toilet. En route, I walked past Tony Adams, who looked at me as if he'd never seen me before in his life, even though he'd been staring at me (and I mean staring) for the last twenty minutes.

I went and had my photograph taken with the two cups, which were on display in an anteroom. Despite my anguish, it was a special moment for me to touch these famous pieces of football silverware: the FA Cup and the League Cup. Billy Bremner had lifted these for Leeds United twenty-one and twenty-five years ago, respectively. My spirits were restored.

And then Ian Wright found me!

He was known as 'Wrighty' to the fans in that highly inventive way that football fans have of making a player sound like one of their own by putting an 'e' sound on the end of their surname. To the players, however, he was known by a shortened version of his first name. You can't get a much shorter name than 'Ian', but Ian Wright was known as 'EE'.

'EE' was so full of praise. I was 'amazing', 'awesome', 'the guv'nor'.

After a few minutes of wallowing, I chanced my arm with him. Here was my opportunity to show Ronni what football could do; a chance to do something she'd love me for again.

'Ian, my girlfriend is a teacher at a school in Holloway . . .'

'Yeah, man.'

'. . . and the boys there are mad on Arsenal and Spurs . . .'

'Spurs? Spurs? Who are they?!'

'Yeah, sorry, well, everything to do with football, really. And I was wondering, would you consider going in and talking to them at some time?'

'Sure, man. Love to. Just give my man Jonty a call and he'll sort it, yeah?'

'Seriously?'

'Seriously. Look!' he said to anyone who was within earshot (which, when Ian Wright is talking, is usually a lot of people). 'He doesn't believe me! I'll be there, man. I know that place; I'll go into the school for your girlfriend. Sure! I love doing that stuff, man!'

As soon as I got home, before I even took off my dinner suit, I told Ronni what had happened. She was thrilled. Ian Wright – the Ian Wright, Wrighty – was going to come and talk to her boys.

'Everyone has commitments though, Ronni. "EE" gets lots of requests,' I said. 'Nothing's final till it's final. You and

I have both had to let people down in the past with gigs and charity things and . . .'

'But he said he'd come, Ali?'

'He said he would.'

'But when?' she asked me.

A few days later, I rang Jonty. I told him I'd spoken to Wrighty about going to my girlfriend's school. Would he actually do it?

'If he said he will, he will. Ian does a lot for charity. People never know about that. They think footballers just train, play, take the money and piss off and play golf. They do so much for charities and communities, and no one ever knows about it. No one ever writes about the good stuff, do they?'

'No, I suppose it doesn't make . . .'

'"EE", right, finishes training and then he'll call me and say, "Where can I go? Where's the hospitals? Who can I help? Give me their names." Seriously, he's such a good man. He'll be there. What's your wife's name?'

'She's my partner.'

'Partner.'

'Ronni.'

'Ronni?'

'Yes, it's short for Veronica.'

'Oh, right, for a minute there I thought . . . you know . . .'

'Oh, no. Ronni's very much a . . .'

'I'll talk to him; we'll sort something out.'

'What did he say?'

'He's sorting it out.'

'What were his exact words?'

How men dread that question! We're all so used to

watching football highlights that that's how we represent conversation – the best bits. Women always want 'their exact words'.

'Jonty will call you.'

'Promise?'

Days went by. No call. Weeks went by. No call.

Ronni then started to badger me again about Wrighty. He was a typical footballer. He wasn't going to come. He was full of empty promises. Jonty probably said that hospital stuff about all the players on his books . . .

Ronni asked me to call Jonty. I did. He said he'd get back to me.

Ronni called Jonty. He'd get back to her.

Ian never went to the school.

Ronni left at the end of the year.

I'm sure 'EE' was very busy. I met him a few years later; he's a nice guy. But, right then, football had let me down. It was at least 1–0 to Ronni.

23

Unkempt and Grumpy

As I sat listening to the radio one morning wondering why, if sex, as they'd just said, was the best form of exercise you can get, there wasn't an area set aside for it in the gym, I realised that I had recently become slightly worried about Alistair.

He was starting to look unkempt and grumpy. He was clearly not himself. Not because of his grumpiness (which is a perfectly natural disposition for him and most of the men in my life, for some reason) but because of the general sense of disarray.

Alistair, as I've mentioned, has always been extremely neat and tidy. It totally intimidated me when we lived together years ago. His books were neat, his toiletries were neat, even his socks were always beautifully folded up and put away in some sort of underwear index system known only to him.

If we had ever compared our respective sock drawers (what a wonderful Bank Holiday that would have been!), it was as if all his socks were living in some perfect, suburban *Stepford Wives* set-up, and mine were squatting in chaos in some dilapidated wing of Miss Havisham's house.

His new-found slovenliness got me thinking: could this habitual, obsessive sense of order correlate with his love of orderly football league tables and results? And, if so, would he totally unravel without them? Would his socks and his brain soon lie untangled on his bedroom floor?

I didn't want that to happen. Alistair has a very defined personality and his need for order is very much a part of that; if this changed, I might not recognise him. And I certainly didn't want to have to go round and fold up his socks – or his cerebral cortex.

As I thought about it more, I realised that almost everything he does has a weird affiliation with football. Even the clothes he doesn't wear that often are segregated into a different area of his wardrobe, waiting for their time in the sun once again, rather like the substitutes sitting on the bench during a match, waiting for their chance.

If I took out the football brick in his wall, he might just totally cave in and crumble. And where would that leave me?

I need organised friends like Ali; they are my lifeblood. They tell me where to meet and when. They help me make decisions. Without them, I might have ended up a sad old recluse sitting in a dusty old wedding dress from a wedding that never happened because no one had told me which church I was meant to be going to.

Perhaps this whole programme was ethically wrong. I might as well be growing an ear on Ali's back as trying to make him give up something so naturally part of him.

Why did I have it in for football so much? I couldn't really explain it. And, in many ways, I know I owe football a debt.

Over the period I have worked with Alistair, most of the successful material we wrote and performed centred around football in some way or other. There is no doubt that football throws up a huge number of world-famous celebrities – probably more than any other sport. And people love to see those celebrities made fun of.

I suppose Ali and I are still most widely known as 'those two impressionists who did Posh and Becks'. Victoria Beckham's lack of understanding of the game, in direct contrast to David's total passion and knowledge of all things football, gave us some great comic ammunition. As did their mutual lack of understanding of lots of things – like the English language.

Everyone always wants to know if Alistair and I ever met Posh and Becks. If I'm out in London, it's the question I get asked most often – after 'Excuse me, lady! Which is way to London Eye?' Well, we didn't. We could have done. But we didn't. We were asked to a party they held at 'Beckingham Palace' on the eve of the 2002 World Cup in South Korea and Japan. They wanted us, we were told, to be there (made up and dressed as them) to introduce all the guests, like latterday town criers, and then to wander round and talk to people as them. We were both keen to go, to see the house, to meet them and to be there. It was to be the social event of the year. But Ali said no. And he was right. He said that, as satirists, if we 'got into bed with' our targets we would be unable to make even gentle fun of them any more. And, on top of that, we were scared they were going to get their own back for a stream of sketches suggesting, among other things, that they thought courgettes were 'hot cucumbers'.

And then there was Sven and Nancy. Sven-Göran Eriksson took over as England manager just after we'd made our first series of *The Big Impression*. His football achievements, however, were soon being overshadowed by the fashions of his long-term girlfriend, Nancy Dell'Olio. With his glasses, slight frame and weak smile Sven was an unlikely looking football manager; Nancy was clearly a passionate, intelligent and, as Ali was always telling me, 'absolutely gorgeous' woman. They were potential comedy gold.

In our sketches, we made Nancy the football brains behind Sven's puppet leader. In our world, he hated football: the game, the players and everything to do with it. In *Sven and Nancy's Big Impression* – a Euro 2004 special – Roman Abramovich kidnaps Nancy until Sven agrees to be manager of his Chelsea team (little knowing that she was the football genius behind all Sven's success). At one point, incarcerated in a cage, Nancy pleads to be let out. She holds a paint chart up to her face and says, 'If my tan drops below Moroccan dusk, I go into seizure!' She was one of the favourite characters I did on the show.

Surprisingly, I found it very enjoyable playing a football expert, and I thought it was very good for Alistair to play the frustrated stooge who couldn't understand or relate to the game at all. The football boot was on the other foot for once.

Years later, I was at a dinner party and, having arrived late, sat down to find Nancy Dell'Olio opposite me. I avoided her gaze at every opportunity by bobbing under the table to retrieve bread rolls, forks and napkins that I had 'dropped'. Much to my relief, she got up to leave before any of the other guests and, as I sunk low in my chair, attempting to be as innocuous as possible, I thought I'd got away with it. Then, I felt an unmistakably well-manicured hand on my shoulder.

'You!' said Nancy.

I gulped and braced myself for an inevitable showdown.

'I want to say one thing to you. Do you know . . .'

'Oh, God,' I thought, 'here it comes.'

'. . . I loved the bit when I was swinging in the cage and I say, "If my tan drop below Moroccan dusk, I go into seizures." It was so funny!'

And so she went on. Not only did she quote almost verbatim that whole sketch, she quoted several others! I was amazed she had seen any of them and I couldn't resist asking her what Sven thought of it all. 'Oh, no!' she exclaimed, 'I would never let *him* see any of it.'

So I have some fond memories from the world of football. Maybe I was being too hard on Ali. I hadn't wanted to ruin his life; I'd wanted to improve it. Maybe I should stop the programme. I hadn't wanted to take chunks of him away; I'd just wanted to add to him. And, above all, this programme was really hard work. I still hadn't worked out the whole twelve steps, for a start. I had the passion, but what is passion without concentration? I was pretending to be something I wasn't. He'd see through it all soon. I could easily just call it all off. Yes, I would. I'd call Ali and tell him. Knowing him, he'll probably be disappointed; once he's started something, he has to finish it. I picked up the phone.

At that moment, there was a report on the radio about crowd trouble after a European match in Manchester. Some fans had beaten up a policeman who had got separated from the rest of his squad, and like lions with an antelope, they had been ready to tear him to pieces. It was horrible. No! I didn't want Ali to have anything to do with this sport any more.

I put the phone down and the television on. Lorraine Kelly. She'd take my mind off it with stories of useless make-overs and models wearing cheap frocks. But, no!

Not today. Lorraine Kelly is talking about *football*!

Oh, okay, it's about how women could survive the onslaught of football that was about to hit our screens, as it does every summer in a year that ends with an even number.

Euro 2006. Ummm . . . I didn't know about this tournament. But I bet Ali did. If it wasn't on my hit list, he certainly wouldn't tell me about it. He'd be trying to sneakily get his football fix from something I didn't know about.

Suddenly, the sanity of women around the country was more important than Ali's sock drawer. Besides, if I did lose him as a friend, I had plenty of other neat female friends around who would keep me ordered and save me from being eaten by silk worms and spiders.

I reached for the phone again. Where had I put it? Where? There.

24

Summer's Coming

The phone was ringing somewhere. Somewhere. Where?
There.

'Ronni?'

'You sound awful, Ali. What's the matter?'

'It's half past nine . . .'

'Yes . . .?'

'It's half past nine.'

'And I've been up for four hours. You have no idea what
it's like having children, do you?'

'It's half past nine.'

'Ali, stop telling me what time it is.'

'But it's . . .'

'Half past nine, I know!'

'Ronni, I don't get in till after midnight doing the show,
and then I like to sit up and watch a bit of telly and . . .'

'Why haven't I heard about Euro 2006?'

'Because it's Euro 2008.'

'Oh, God! Is it 2008?'

'Yes.'

'No wonder the dentist keeps ringing me to make an
appointment.'

'Anyway, it's weeks away.'

'Well, I know it's a really big tournament, Ali, and everyone will be watching it and it's only once every four years
and you're really looking forward to it and probably already
have a wall chart and a sticker collection and all sorts of

memories of childhood experiences about similar tournaments in Belgium or wherever and it's not on my programme because I didn't know about it, but I'm sorry, Ali,
Euro 2006 . . .'

'2008.'

'2008 is history as far as you're concerned.'

'It's history as far as you're concerned.'

'What?'

'Look, Ronni. Can you call me back? It's too early for
this.'

'Oh, God. All right. When?'

'I don't know. In a couple of hours?'

'You lucky bastard!'

'Bye, Ronni.'

It was probably time I got up but I couldn't handle Ronni
yet. I didn't want her eating away at even more of me. I put
the radio on. There was something on 5 Live about a group
of Rangers fans attacking a policeman in Manchester. It
was horrible. They ended the bulletin with a piece about
sex being the best form of exercise you can get. Hum!
Handy. After the usual breakfast, I cycle to the gym. I've got
a session with my personal trainer – a gorgeous Greek
Australian. We normally do a mixture of circuit training, free
weights, machines and kinesis. Maybe I should tell her
what I heard on the news . . .

As I head back to the changing rooms to swap gym gear
for swimming trunks, the phone goes in my locker. Ronni's
number. To turn Ronni down once is difficult; to turn her
down twice is impossible.

'Hello, Ronni.'

'You know, I started to feel sorry for you last night.'

148

'Why?'

'I thought maybe this wasn't fair, this whole idea. The programme. But this policeman thing in Manchester . . . it's horrible.'

'I know but . . .'

'So no Euro 2008.'

'I wasn't actually going to watch it anyway, Ronni.'

'Really? Oh, well done! I'm so proud of you! Is that because of my influence?'

'No. England didn't qualify. It was going to be my protest against Steve McClaren.'

'Who?'

'The manager who didn't get us there and . . . oh, it doesn't matter.'

'Why is it all echo-y?'

'What?'

'The phone sounds all echo-y. Are you on the toilet reading about football?'

'No! I'm at the gym. In the changing room.'

'Oh, good. Anyway, I've got to go. One of my girls is scribbling on the other one's face with an indelible marker.'

Once Ronni had gone, I heard what I thought was a trailer for a forthcoming Sky football match on one of the wallpaper televisions in the changing room. As I cheated a look at the screen, I saw that it wasn't a football trailer; it was a trailer for Mitchell and Webb, in which David Mitchell – or was it Robert Webb? – was spoofing the endless Sky football trailers. It went something like:

Catch all the constantly happening football here! Yes, the football never ends . . . Tonight, two more teams will play football . . . and this weekend a clash of two more teams . . .! We've got thousands and thousands of hours of football! . . . It's impossible to keep track of all the football but your best chance is here . . . Every kick of it massively mattering to someone presumably! . . . It will never stop; it will never be decided who has finally won the football . . . The football never ends . . . Everything to play for and for ever to play it in! It never ends . . .

I was completely arrested by the sketch. It was so true. Football didn't ever end. It was a cycle. Season after season. No one ever actually ultimately wins. On it goes. It is an addiction. A drug. And Sky, more than anyone else, were the pushers.

The sketch summed up everything Ronni had been saying about football on television and football in general. I thought I wouldn't tell her about it or she'd learn it and quote it at me and everyone she knows who likes football for ever after.

'It never ends.' 'There is no winner.' And it certainly doesn't belong in the summer. By not reading about football, about Euro 2008, I hadn't whetted my appetite for the tournament. When the press puts little stories your way about what might be and what what-might-be might mean for this player or that player's wife or child or team-mate or ex-team-mate, you need to know the answer, the outcome. I'd broken the chain. I no longer needed answers to questions that didn't matter. For the first time ever (and not just because of England's absence), I determined that I would not watch, listen to or talk about one single second of a major summer football tournament. Not one match. No analysis. Nothing. I was almost excited by the prospect of my ignorance.

I felt clean.

I threw my used gym things into the locker without even thinking about neatly folding them up, I put my swimming trunks on and headed for the pool.

25

A Frontal Lobotomy without the Anaesthetic

Step Nine: Turn Off His Radio

With renewed vigour after my momentary lapse, I have agreed to meet Alistair in Holland Park. It's a Sunday – a theatre-free day for Ali – and the sun is shining. We can lie in the sun. Ali loves to lie in the sun. He goes brown very quickly because of his Indian roots.

He discovered this Indian connection a few years ago while doing *Who Do You Think You Are?* He was astonished. I could have told him he had Indian blood the day I met his father and saved Ali a trip to India, and the BBC a lot of work; it was obvious, I thought. If only he listened to me more.

I, however, don't tan at all. After a week in the sun I usually reach a warm shade of 'pale'. I have legs the colour of milk bottles. I figure by lying in the sun I might take his mind off football more easily; his tan-ity vanity will take over again.

I am running a little late. As I reach our spot in the park, Ali is already waiting for me, watching a group of dads and lads having a kick around.

'I wasn't really watching it, I was just . . .'

'I think glancing at a bit of innocent football in the park is okay, Ali. Anyway, today isn't about making you give up watching any more football.'

'Oh, that's nice!'

'Today's step is about giving up listening to it.'

'What?!'

'No more radio, Ali.'

Ali was silent. Well, that was easier than I thought. But then he just stared at me like I'd threatened his young.

'Why are you staring at me like that?'

'I didn't think you'd remember radio.'

'Of course.'

'Dammit!'

'Did you only agree to do this because you thought I'd inadvertently leave things out?'

'No.'

'You did, didn't you?'

'No. It's just . . .'

'You have no idea how infuriated football makes me, do you?'

'I do. It's just . . .'

'I've done my research.'

'I'm starting to see that.'

'No more radio, Ali.'

'But, Ronni, some of my earliest memories are of listening to football on the radio! *Sports Report* is the very sound of order and everything being all right with the world.'

I'd clearly hit a nerve. 'Shall we sit down?'

Ali sits on the grass in a daze, not even checking to see what he may be about to sit in.

'James Alexander Gordon . . .'

'What whattie whosit?'

'The man who reads the football results . . .'

'Oh.'

'. . . is the very fabric of our nation, Ronni!'

153

'He sounds to me like he should have invented something. "James Alexander Gordon, he gave us Bakelite – or a field transistor for the army."'

'Well, he didn't. He reads the football results every Saturday on Radio 5 Live. At 5 p.m.'

And Ali starts singing what I can only assume is the theme tune. I hope his singing's better in *Cabaret*.

'My dad and I used to speak along with him in the car on the way back from Coventry.'

'Right. Well, I'm very sorry but . . .'

'You see, you could guess the number of goals the away team had scored by the cadence of James Alexander Gordon's voice as he read the home team's score.'

'I'm sure that's very sweet, Ali, but . . .'

'If the home team had scored one goal and you could tell from the music of James Alexander Gordon's voice that the away team hadn't scored, Dad would jump in and replace James Alexander Gordon's "nil" with "lost".'

'Really?'

'"Liverpool one . . . Southampton . . . lost." The first time he did it, I thought it was hilarious.'

'I'm sure.'

'It went on for thirty years.'

Last week, this charming little story might have made me doubt myself, but now I was a woman on a mission again.

'Well, I'm sorry, Ali, but . . .'

'Ronni, listening to sport on the radio is part of our culture, part of our history. I can't . . .'

'Ali, the results on the radio are bad enough. But the commentary? Come on! How can that be exciting? You can't see anything! You don't know what's happening!'

'I know! And it's more exciting precisely *because* you can't see what's happening – like having sex blindfolded.'

I frown at him.

'Probably,' he adds, a little too quickly.

I won't push it. He seems wired today. Is it the coming-off-football delirium tremens? Or has he got in with a bad crowd?

I distract him with another question and some metaphorical cat-stroking.

'How are you getting on without the Sunday papers, by the way?'

'It's okay. I don't *need* to read the reports, you're right.'

'Good, well done!'

'And I still have *Match of the Day*, so I at least see the Premier League games and tables. And the attendances are on the straplines after each game. But I do feel desperate for the full tables. Desperate! It's the first thing I always did on a Sunday: cereal and scores, then toast and tables . . .'

'God! It even alliterates. What do you have with the attendances?'

'A shit, normally.'

'Classy.'

'And I really want to know all the other attendances, Ronni. It's weird,' he said, his leg twitching uncontrollably.

'Look at the beautiful day, Ali. The first really sunny day of the summer. The blossom's out and people are wandering around and smiling without needing to know the attendance yesterday at Everton v. Ipswich. They cope without it.'

'Everton wouldn't play Ipswich; they're in different divisions.'

'It could have been in the cups!'

'No. They both got knocked out of the FA Cup in the earlier rounds: Everton lost to Oldham at home and Ipswich lost . . .'

'Ali! This is exactly why you need to give all this up. Think of all the other things you can do today . . .'

'Yeah, like meet you and have more of my life taken away.'

'No! Have more of your life opened up. As a woman, do you know how attractive it is if a man isn't obsessed with football and all its minutiae?'

Ali scuffs the ground with the toe of his shoe.

'Shall we get an ice cream?'

'Okay.'

As we queue by the ice-cream van, Ali moans about the exhaust fumes from the ever-running engine.

'Small children,' he says, just a little too loudly, 'all they want is an ice cream, and they end up with lungs full of benzene and carbon monoxide! But do the government put a warning on the side of every ice-cream van: "Buying ice cream kills children" . . .?'

People are starting to look round. Is this what he's going to replace football with? Is this what he's going to be like? An eco-terrorist?

'Well, do they?'

'No,' I answer quickly.

'No. There must be a more environmentally friendly way of chilling ice cream. The ice-cream van, for me, is a microcosm of the destruction of the environment: the children are ignorant humanity standing looking pollution in the face, the ice cream is our greed, and the van is industry, continuously polluting and killing our children without a care.'

'Shall we just get a cup of tea instead?'

At the cafe, Ali calms down a little but he's still talking at ninety miles an hour.

'Okay. The main difficulty for me with this programme of yours, Ronni, is that this is the busiest time of the year for football – the business end of the season. Now, in May, all the games are really important, really exciting. They really matter. Play-off finals, cup finals, the Champions League final – it's Man United and Chelsea, on Wednesday.'

'How do you know?!'

'A taxi driver told me. I tried to stop him but . . .'

'Okay. I believe you. But look, Ali, there's no good time to give up; there's always a big game coming up – it always matters. Or that's what you think. But it doesn't matter. Are you listening to me?'

Ali nods feverishly.

'None of it really matters. And, if you can give up now, at the end of a season, just think how easy it'll make giving up for good. You can't come off the programme now just because you've seen some dads and lads having a kick around and it made you think of . . .'

'Okay. I'll stop listening to it on the radio,' he says, interrupting me rudely.

'And you don't play any more, do you?'

'No.'

'Good, because I would have had to stop that too. So two steps in one again. We're doing well. See how organised I am?'

'Yes. Clinical. I'm impressed. What number step are we up to now then on your list?'

'Ermmm . . .'

One Big Turn-Off

Later that day, I reluctantly move my radio from its regular set-ting on 5 Live to Virgin (now Absolute) Radio. I thought it was going to hurt, but it was good to hear music after years of the jokey, blokey seriousness of 5 Live, and I liked their playlist.

Virgin/Absolute also boast a 'No repeat 9–5' policy, which means, it seems, that unlike other stations, Virgin/Absolute don't play the same song within that 9–5 period. Great, I thought! That, after all, would be torture – to hear the same song more than once in an eight-hour period. Well done, Virgin/Absolute Radio!

What they do do, I soon notice, is play a trailer every twenty minutes telling me about their 'No repeat 9–5' pol-icy. A trailer which becomes so annoying that it makes me think, 'Would I rather hear the same record twice in an eight-hour period and risk the psychological torture that may entail or would I rather hear the repeated "No repeat 9–5" policy boast every twenty minutes?

'You don't get this on 5 Live,' I thought. After two days of repeated 'No repeat's, I get so annoyed I switch to Classic FM.

Classic FM is wonderful. Well, at first it's wonderful – if I can just ignore the adverts and the fact that they seem to just play the same things every week in a different order. And the fact that people keep ringing in to request bits of 'lovely' music and telling you what they're doing on their 'lovely' little days . . .

'Hello, Jane. My husband and I are just painting the shed and were wondering if you could play us the lovely British Airways music sung by the lovely Katherine Jenkins . . .'

'Hello, Jamie. My lovely wife and I are just driving up the lovely M4 to pick up our lovely daughter from lovely Keele University. She's just finished her first year doing Mechanical Engineering and we'd love to hear the lovely "Nessun Dorma" sung by the lovely Katherine Jenkins . . .'

I'm tempted to ring in and say, 'Hello, Jamie. I'm just having sex in the kitchen with a fabulously dirty girl I've just met, and she said, "Wouldn't it be nice to do it to a bit of Erik Satie?" Could you oblige? Many thanks.'

But I can't ignore all these things about Classic FM, so then I turn to Radio 3, which plays classical music without all the fanfares and the back-patting, and even though it does get a bit operatic and discordant at times, there isn't any of that cheesy smiling. Hooray! This is my station of the future! And if I do get irritated, I can pop along the dial to Radio 4 for a while and learn things about the world.

And both Radio 3 and Radio 4 are completely football-free zones: there's no hint of a score or a match report or a forthcoming fixture (except from Garry Richardson on Radio 4's *Today* programme but, as I'm never up before nine anyway, he won't be a problem). And on Radio 3 they don't even mention football on the news. If England won the World Cup, they still probably wouldn't mention it – unless Simon Rattle scored the winning goal.

I would be better informed here, I thought. And happier. And I was. Principally because I was no longer listening to people moaning. People don't really moan on Radio 3 or Radio 4; they just 'get on with things' (except for John Humphrys on the *Today* programme, obviously, but, as I'm never up before nine anyway, he won't be a problem).

In hindsight, I realise that the endless football phone-ins on 5 Live were just full of unhappy people moaning. Moaning about referees, managers, players, their own fans, other fans, ticket prices, shirt prices, programme prices, policing, commentators, the previous caller, Alan Green, the next caller, last week's caller, trains, coaches, roads, car parks, parks football, Queens Park Rangers, Queen of the South, Southampton, Northampton, Preston North End . . . endless, pointless, feckless, fecking moaning.

Football clearly didn't make men happier. More often than not, it made them miserable. And their misery had been making me miserable. I hadn't realised it but I suppose I'd always wanted to say to these people, 'Ah, get a life!'

Thanks to Ronni, I was getting one. And it felt, and sounded, good!

27

Chorizo Sausages

Step Ten: Get Him to Hang Up His Boots

I was beginning to think that my obsession with making Ali give up football meant that I was now equally addicted to football, albeit in a different way. It was all I could think and talk about suddenly. Why did men love it so much? Why had I never been able to understand their obsessional nature? Not just about football but about anything. Maybe I'm naive where men are concerned – which is odd, because I do come from a very male family.

I never usually use that term. After all, what does being from a very male family mean? That even your mother was a small balding man called Tony?

I had two elder brothers and, along with my father, they were very much men's men (obsessed with cars, trains and Airfix models), but I don't remember them ever having a particular passion for football. But then there wasn't as much football on television in those days. And even if there had been, I don't think my very male family would have particularly wanted to watch it. Or been able to. We had a big old black-and-white telly. Once you'd switched it on, it took so long to warm up that you would either get distracted by something else or forget that you had switched it on in the first place.

So maybe I grew up underestimating the importance of football to men. Also Troon, the town where I grew up, was so consumed by the sport of golf that it was as if no other sport existed. Despite being quite small, Troon had several golf courses. We even lived on Golf Crescent – opposite a golf course. I was psychologically scarred because we were the only family in the town not to play golf. Or so it seemed.

The golf course opposite our house had a little box with a woman in it who regularly shouted through a tannoy at 6 a.m. in the morning, 'Mr McTavish, your balls are ready!' I have an enduring memory of my father marching across the road in his pyjamas, shouting, 'Will you shut up, woman!' This did not help our cause. After this, I was half expecting to have offensive golfing slogans daubed on our front door.

The players would even be out in the winter, in the snow, playing with their little red balls. Such all-consuming passion for a sport confused me, even disturbed me. I slightly changed my opinion when the British Open was played in the town and we took in a golfer as a lodger, as most inhabitants did. He was a fat little Belgian man who ran around in his Y-fronts and gave me, *me*, a box of Terry's All Gold chocolates. A big box. It was the most exciting thing that had happened to me. (Remember this was in the 1970s, when the concept of a treat was a bowl of Angel Delight on a wet caravanning holiday or going to somebody's house who had a SodaStream.)

But, because we didn't play golf, we weren't interested in watching the sport. If you do play a sport, generally one of the reasons why you watch that sport being played by professionals is to learn from them. So, if you suggest to your partner that he no longer plays football, chances are you will lessen his desire to watch football.

However, a boyfriend/husband who plays football

should not be discouraged from playing if you are a WAG and, by playing football, your boyfriend/husband is earning copious amounts of money for you to dispose of in the manner you've grown accustomed to. In fact, if you are the WAG of a famous footballer, this book is really not for you at all (I should probably have pointed that out earlier). Although if you are the WAG of a famous footballer, you probably put the book down as soon as you realised there weren't any pictures of handbags in it.

Playing football in itself is not necessarily such a bad thing. Alistair played in goal. I went to watch him play once; I thought it was only proper. I'd never had a boyfriend who played football – it was what they call on BBC2 arts programmes 'a rite of passage'. I thought it would be like something out of a Woody Allen film; but then I think everything in life is going to be like a Woody Allen film and it never is. In fact, I've begun to think not even Woody Allen films are like Woody Allen films any more.

So I imagined lots of long-haired girlfriends with brown scarves and big coats, cradling coffees in paper cups between their hands and with a copy of a second-hand Steinbeck novel peeking out of their coat pockets. I imagined artistic men standing, chuckling, alongside them or sitting next to them on wooden benches in little stands. And the relevant boyfriends looking over every so often from the field of play at the relevant girlfriends and waving.

There was none of this. It was just me, standing by a lot of cheap sports bags, discarded plastic drinks bottles and strange bits of tape.

I was cold, damp and very bored, but I was doing my bit

for my fella. I shouted 'Come on, Ali!' every now and again, but everyone looked at me like I was three years old.

Ali looked fit in his kit. The other lads in his team didn't look that fit. Some of them didn't look like they'd ever been fit. And what is it about polyester shirts that makes them cling to every bulge? And their shorts were tiny back then. I remember noticing that everyone's privates were being cut in two by the front seams; I've never been able to look at a chorizo in the same way since.

He picked up an injury – nothing nasty, but enough for me to have to carry his bag home and then supply him with sympathy and various sources of heat and ice all afternoon.

I asked him why he did it; was it worth the bother?

'What would I do without it?' he said.

And that's always it, in the end, isn't it? What would they do without it?

But I don't have to get Ali to stop playing as part of the programme because he picked up a really bad injury one day, when he was in his early thirties, and that was that; he ruptured a knee or something and hasn't played since. In fact, his interest in the game definitely waned when he was no longer playing. As he was unable to copy what he'd seen David Seaman do, he was less interested in watching David Seaman do what David Seaman did.

And because Ali is no longer playing, I can move on to the next step. And the next step is a biggie, possibly the biggest step so far: giving up *Match of the Day*. He's going to need some soft-soaping. I call him.

'Ali.'

'Ronni.'

'Meet me at Le Maison de Juliette at one . . .'

'What?'

'Meet me at one o'clock, at Le Maison de Juliette!'

'It's *La* Maison . . .'

'Just meet me there!'

28

The Catch-Up . . .

Step Eleven: Tell Him Match of the Day Has Had Its Day

I sit and wait for Ronni at La Maison de Juliette, a restaurant in west London. It's what some people might call a 'posh' restaurant.

I don't like the word 'posh'. It's bandied around far too easily these days and has about as much meaning now as (so we were told in the 1970s) the word 'nice' had. Back then, we were always being told not to use the word 'nice' – 'It is bland and signifies nothing,' said teachers and 'posh' friends' parents.

Now, however, 'nice' seems to be much more acceptable, perhaps because fewer things are 'nice'. So many things are depressing and dark and worrying and 'awesome' and 'wicked' and 'bad' and 'crucial' and 'genius' and 'minging' that poor little 'nice', lucky old 'nice' has come back into use. It means something again – which is nice.

'Posh', however, has come to mean a hundred things: 'exclusive', 'old-fashioned', 'not very male', 'not having an accent', 'someone with a modicum of manners', 'clean', 'tidy', 'not covered in litter and graffiti' . . . and Victoria Beckham.

Anyway, in the case of the restaurant where I wait for Ronni, it means white linen tablecloths and menus written on small blackboards in French writing.

Why do all French people have the same handwriting? It's such an identifiable style, isn't it? They write like no one else and they all write the same. It must make being a police graphologist in France a total nightmare: '*Oui, inspecteur*, we have analysed the handwriting of the murderer and narrowed down the list of suspects to just . . . everyone in France.'

A million thoughts run through my head as I wait for Ronni to arrive. She's late. She's always late. I thought I was bad at being late – or good at being late, I suppose – but Ronni really takes the biscuit, the posh biscuit, the French biscuit, '*le biscuit snob*' . . .

Suddenly, there is a blur of black hair and grimaces and coats and bags outside, and the heavy glass door yanks open.

'Hi, Ali! I'm so sorry. I'm late. I know. I just couldn't . . . Oh, you don't want to know . . .'

This sentence from Ronni normally means that there is no reason for her lateness, except bad time-keeping. Or children doing something they shouldn't. Normally with their bodily functions. In which case she's right, I don't want to know.

'It was the children. Poor little mites. They both had the most terrible tummy bug and awful . . .'

'It's fine, Ronni. I was . . .'

'You really have no idea what it's like . . .'

'Well, I sort of do now, really.'

'So how's it all going?'

'Well . . .'

'Have you ordered yet?'

'No, I was waiting for you.'

'You should have ordered,' says Ronni, scouring the

menu, her head twitching in tiny, keen little movements –
like a cat watching a fruit fly.

I knew if I had ordered she would have told me I was
rude and should have waited for her.

'Anyway,' I continue, 'it's been difficult – especially the
not reading about football bit. D'you know, I realised that
I'd been reading about football since I was . . .'

'I think I'll have the fish.'

'. . . about seven years old. So that's been . . .'

'The fish here is really good.'

'. . . that's been a shock but you know . . .'

'Oh, but the chicken looks lovely!'

I decide to stop answering Ronni's question until she's
actually listening to me.

'Excuse me, sir!'

She calls a waiter over. She always calls waiters 'sir'. I'm
not sure if she does this knowing that nobody else calls
waiters 'sir' in an effort to make them feel spoilt or whether
she does this *not* knowing that nobody else calls waiters
'sir'. I suppose I should ask her but then she might stop
doing it, and it is strangely charming – like Ronni herself.

'Sir, is your chicken nice?'

Another typical Ronni-ism. How many waiters or wait-
resses are ever going to say that their chicken isn't nice?
'No, it's nothing special. Actually, if I were you, I'd go next
door to the little cafe and have the bacon and egg for
£2.50. You're basically just paying for the tablecloths and
the French writing here.'

'Yes,' he says, 'it comes with chips and a small salad.'

'Oh, could I have it without the chips . . .'

'Yes, madam.'

'. . . but with a lot of salad?'

'Yes, madam.'

'In fact, could I just have a big salad without the chicken?'

'We don't do salads.'

'But you do a side salad with the chicken. So can I just have a really big side salad with a bit of chicken?'

'Then it's not a side salad, madam.'

I want to die.

'I know, sir, but I don't want to eat a lot of chicken, you see, because I'm trying . . .'

. . . to be awkward . . .?

'. . . to lose a bit of . . . well, you know. Ali, what are you having?'

'Can I have the fish stew?'

'Ooh, that sounds nice. Where's that?'

The waiter points it out on the menu, clearly resisting the temptation to say, 'There. Where it says "fish stew".'

'Umm, can I have that too, please, sir?'

'Yes, madam.'

'Does it come with any salad?'

'No, madam. But I can get you a side salad, if you like.'

'Yes, please, sir. But can you make sure there are no onions in the salad?'

'There are no onions in the salad, madam.'

'And no beetroot.'

'There's no beetroot in the salad, madam.'

'And can you make sure there's quite a lot of leaves because the last time I ate here you only gave me two leaves of lettuce. It was like a serving suggestion on a packet of Ryvita.'

'I'll make sure there's lots of lettuce for you, madam.'

'And when you say "lettuce" it's not lettuce like my gran

used to grow in her garden in Herne Bay, is it? It's proper crunchy leaves from round the world . . .'

'I think it's from Worcestershire.'

'Oh, that'll be fine. And will it be charged as a side salad or are you very kindly, sir, offering me a bit of salad on the side?'

'I have to charge it as a side salad, madam.'

'Oh. But I don't really want a side salad.'

'But, madam, I thought you said . . .'

'I just want a bit of salad on the side.'

'I have to charge it as a side salad.'

'But . . .'

'It's fine, Ronni! I'll pay.'

'It's not about that. I just think, sir . . .'

'And one side salad!' I say, to keep the peace. 'Thank you. Sir.'

'Thank *you*, sir. And drinks for yourselves?'

'I'll have . . . what are you having, Ali?'

'An apple juice with no ice. And no straw. Thanks.'

'You're so fussy! Listen to him! He's so fussy!'

'Madam?'

'Yes?'

'To drink?'

'Oh, I'll have some fizzy water, please, sir.'

'One sparkling . . .'

'Is your fizzy water fizzy or is it Badoit? Because that says it's fizzy and it's not actually fizzy; it's like it's been left by the bed for three days.'

'It's San Pellegrino.'

'Great. Yes. I'll have that.'

'Thank you, sir. Madam.'

'There. That was easy. So how's it all going . . .?'

'Well, pretty well. I'm not missing watching it live because I still have *Match of the Day* . . .'

'A-ha . . .'

'And I'm not missing listening to Five Live because I'm really enjoying listening to Radio 4!'

'That's good!'

'Except for *Gardeners' Question Time*.'

'It helps if you have a garden.'

'Yes. And *You and Yours*.'

'Yes. But otherwise . . .'

'Oh! Brilliant! Yeah. But I do find it really hard reading the paper from the front to the back.'

'Maybe you'll get used to that in time.'

'And even harder stopping before the sport. It feels like I'm ignoring an old friend . . .'

'Oh, you've reminded me I must ring Claire . . . Sorry, yes?'

'But most of all I miss . . .'

'Do you think they'll put dressing on the salad?'

'Probably.'

'I don't want dressing.'

'Then probably not.'

'Good. Yes. Go on.'

'Well, I miss looking forward to something, I suppose.'

'Right.'

'And the sense of hope.'

'Hope?'

'Yes. Hope.'

'Why hope?'

'Football's all about hope really. You hope your team's going to win against all odds, you hope this team is going to escape relegation, you hope Man United won't win everything again . . .'

'And that's what football fans are addicted to?'

'Yes. Having something to look forward to, to define the week. And hope. Above all, the hope that it may be better this time. That your team will suddenly be brilliant. And you don't want to miss it if they are.'

'Hope?'

'Hope. It's very powerful. As Shakespeare said, "The miserable have no other medicine but only hope."'

'That was before valium, obviously.'

'Well, yes.'

'But surely after years of perpetual disappointment, Ali, with Leeds and Coventry and all the other teams that you've supported "till you die", – Ronni did the inverted commas again, not realising that people stopped doing that in 1992 – 'you should all see that all that "hoping" doesn't make sense. All that "hoping" still hasn't got Rochdale into the Premier League, has it? It's all about the hope of something existing which probably can't exist – as much as you might want it to.'

'Like your chicken salad.'

'Yes.'

'Sorry. What do you mean?'

'Well, think about it: there's not enough success to go round, is there? Not enough potential success to satisfy the hope.'

'Yeah, but even so . . .'

'No, listen to me: only one team can win the Premier League, yes?'

'Yes . . .'

'Only one team can win the FA Cup, yes?'

'Yes.'

'Only one team can win that other cup. Only one team

can win the Champions League. And three other teams can win the divisions they're in, right?'

'I'm impressed, Ronni.'

'Thank you. Now, how many teams are there all together – about? Just roughly?'

'Ninety-two.'

'How do you know that?'

'Everyone knows that. At one point, I wanted to become part of the "92 Club".'

'What's that? If it's about female conquests, I don't want to know.'

'No. It's about going to see a game at all ninety-two football grounds . . .'

'God! How crashingly dull! So, anyway, if we subtract the maximum number of – what was it? – seven winners . . .'

'Yes, seven. Presuming that a different club wins each of the tournaments . . .'

'Yes, presuming that. So, seven from ninety-two. What's that? Eighty-six?'

'Eighty-five.'

'Eighty-five. Then eighty-five sets of supporters and players nationwide will be disappointed every year. That's a very large percentage of the country being disappointed at the same time.'

'Like when Coldplay released *X and Y*.'

'Ali! That was a great album.'

'Well . . .'

'But don't you see? Believing in a team's success is fantastical.'

'But isn't that a good thing?'

'Why?'

'Well, because then men always have something to

174

look forward to. The next game. The next season. They always have hope! I bet if you compared suicide rates among men who are football fans and women in . . .'

'What's that got to do with anything?'

'Well, I bet you that you'd find far fewer football fans suffer from bouts of depression.'

'Yes, because they're *permanently* depressed. By Spurs. Or Arsenal. Or whoever it is – except Manchester United.'

'No, they're permanently *hopeful*! And that's what I miss most, to answer your question.'

'What was my question?'

'How's it all going?'

'Right. Good. Yes.'

'And, even if you could prove that hope is ultimately nearly always doomed, you've still go to battle that other great pillar of the football community . . .'

'Alex Ferguson?'

'No.'

'John Motson?'

'No. Listen to me!'

'Sorry.'

'Tradition.'

'Oh, tradition is just a posh word for "habit". And "hope" is just habit too.'

'Is it?'

'Yes. As long as you apply logic to football, Ali, and start to ask yourself a few simple questions, you'll chip away at the wall that football creates around its little city.'

'What wall?'

'The wall which is made principally from lack of reason, lack of thought and lack of logic. Once logic enters into football, you see the game from a woman's point of view. You see that football doesn't really make sense. It's just habit.'

I was beaten. Suddenly, the waiter was at my left shoulder, placing food on our rather small table.

'Two fish stews and one salad . . .?'

'Thank you.'

Just as he was turning to leave, Ronni was at it again.

'Excuse me, sir?'

'Yes, madam?'

'Could I have a bit more lettuce?'

Before he had time to sigh, she hit me with the big one.

'Now, are you ready to give up *Match of the Day*?'

29

Men and Women

Step Twelve: Tell Him to Stop Lying!

Oh, God! 'At the end of the day' maybe men really do need football. The refuge of football. Whether it's the single refuge of *Match of the Day* or the double refuge of the newspaper on the toilet behind the closed bathroom door.

Seeing Ali crumble in the restaurant has brought my doubts on again. It felt so good, but at the same time so bad – like watching *Cash in the Attic*! I pace around the kitchen, trying my best to clean up some fuzzy felt animals that my children really don't have the passion for that I did.

Basically, by opening all this up, I've started to think that . . . well, I'm just not sure how much men and women actually like each other.

Love each other? Yes.

Attracted to each other? Tick.

But actually like each other in a 'let's-have-a-real-laugh-about-the-things-we-have-in-common-over-a-bottle-of-wine-and-a-bowl-of-tortilla-chips-while-watching-*Ugly-Betty*' way? Well, the jury's out on that one.

It would help if we wanted to do the same things. And if we were more honest with each other. Most conversations with your partner are some weird form of doublespeak. Certainly, what men say and what they are actually thinking are two very different things. Especially where football is concerned.

HE SAYS	HE MEANS
No, you go out, darling. They're more your friends than mine, anyway.	I want to watch the football.
Why don't you have an early night?	I want to watch the football.
You look gorgeous; have you lost weight?	Can I watch the football?
I thought you didn't want to celebrate your birthday.	There's a game on tomorrow night – and I've got tickets!
Push, darling! Push!	When would be the best time to check the scores?

And, sadly, they think they're getting away with it, but we know what their doublespeak means every time!

HE SAYS	SHE THINKS
No, you go out, darling. They're more your friends than mine, anyway.	He wants to watch the football.
I'll babysit; you go and have a good time. You deserve it!	He wants to watch the football.
Push, darling! Push!	I bet the real father wouldn't want to check the scores.

Football makes people lie, just like any other addiction: the smoker with the minty breath; the alcoholic with the starey-eyed denials; the drug addict asking for money for chocolate. Addiction breeds dishonesty. Dishonesty breaks up relationships. It is *never* a good thing to lie!

My husband comes into the kitchen. He's finally noticed all the self-help books. I say I've got them as early Christmas presents for friends. It seems to keep him happy.

I must keep going with Ali. He is doing well. The wired stage has passed. He seems happy. Deep down, he really does seem happier.

30

Bye-Bye, Alan!

Oh, God! *Match of the Day*. She wants me to give up *Match of the Day*! Oh, my God! I could cry, I could really, actually cry now! I slump onto the sofa, alone in the dark, empty flat. I clench my fists, dig my nails into my palms and look into the distance. That's supposed to help keep tears away, isn't it? Or is that nausea?

This really is a biggie. *The* biggie. It's the ultimate football programme, everyone knows that. It's steeped in history and tradition. It's all so familiar: the music, the studio, the camerawork, the format, the analysis, the fact that Bolton are always on at the end, the pundits, the jocularity, Goal of the Month . . .

You've had the anticipation on *Football Focus*, the results on *Final Score*, the analysis on the red button and now, on *Match of the Day*, the action and more analysis, analysis to end all analysis – final chord – now go to bed, there is no more football you can take today . . .

Match of the Day has always been the very symbol of Saturday night, the image of football, the cause of the arguments between man and woman, brother and sister, husband and wife. If you missed it, it generally meant you were 'courting' – and happy to make the ultimate sacrifice in pursuit of the ultimate reward. *Match of the Day* for sex.

If you were in a relationship or married, you'd stay at home and bargain to see it – *Match of the Day* for *Casualty*. Or, if you were out together, you'd do all you could to get home in time to see it: lie about 'being tired' or 'not feeling too good', or worrying that you'd left the cat on . . . Either way, life and Saturday night revolved around *Match of the Day*.

But now, sitting on my sofa – perhaps as a result of Ronni's niggling, of her persuasive, pervasive, deadly logic – its flaws are suddenly all drawn to the surface. *Match of the Day* has changed. It used to be an hour long. Now it's an hour and a half long. It's too long. The action from the games has got shorter, the chat has got longer, and the highlights that are shown are shown so many times from so many different angles.

Do I really want to see the goals from Bolton v. Wigan at five minutes to midnight? Do I want to stay up, fighting off tiredness and losing my libido, to see Blackburn's tame winner against Fulham? Am I really bothered that a complete team of foreigners under the name of 'Arsenal' have drawn 0–0 with Aston Villa, in a ground named after an airline?

And the analysis of the pundits is repetitive. Just like the newspapers, it's the same words, the same incidents season after season. Just substitute the names of the players and one or two of the teams and you could watch a recording of Alan Hansen and the boys from three years ago analysing an incident and, but for a few more grey hairs, you wouldn't spot the difference.

I realise that every time I have switched on *MOTD* over the last few years, if I'm honest, I have been hoping to see the Leeds United of the early 1970s playing again. My Leeds. Not one of their old games (which you can sometimes see early in the mornings, I'm told, on Sky3). I had wanted, I realise, to see them playing now. My heroes. Unaged.

Unchanged. Undaunted. Taking on Manchester United and Chelsea and Wigan today. And winning. And winning handsomely. Timeless. Ageless. I had been searching for the seven-year-old, yearning for the time with my dad, hot ears and cold feet in dressing gowns and slippers by an orange two-bar electric fire with a packet of crisps on the side.

Perhaps I don't need Ronni's amateur therapy; I need real therapy. Or perhaps I'm just getting old, thinking that it was all better in my day. That's just part of the ageing process, isn't it? Maybe this whole addiction to football is me trying to return to the paternal womb. And I am not a seahorse. Nor was my dad.

I will give up *Match of the Day*. I hadn't been a regular for some time. And anyway, she didn't say I couldn't watch *Match of the Day 2*!

The phone rings. It's Ronni.

'Oh, and Ali . . .'

'Yes?'

'That goes for *Match of the Day 2* too.'

'Tutu?'

'No. 2. Too. Ta-ta.'

'Ta-ta.'

Dammit. The phone rings again.

'And *Football Focus*.'

'What? No, not yet! Not *Focus* as well . . .'

'Yes, *Focus* as well. Bye!'

Ronni had taken out all of Sky, now she'd taken out all of the BBC. No papers. No radio. No live games. There was nothing left. Except England games! She hadn't mentioned those!

But I was being broken down. Destroyed. Emasculated. Carefully. Cleverly. Systematically.

I thought I'd have some toast before bed. I put the bread in the toaster and opened the cupboard to take out the Marmite in readiness. But my hand paused over the jar and, in front of my very eyes, took out the strawberry jam instead.

31

Meeting Our Victims

Step Thirteen: Giving Up En-ger-land

By my reckoning I'd actually done my twelve steps – even if three of the last four hadn't been on my original list – yet I still had two more to go. But I wasn't sure whether to go ahead with getting Ali to give up England.

Like many women, I enjoy the World Cup – especially if England or Scotland are involved. (I know it's unusual, but I have strong allegiances to both countries. I support both England *and* Scotland – unless they play each other, of course, in which case I support . . . whoever looks like they're going to win.) The World Cup is a different kettle of football fish and has always been the exception to my anti-football rule. Suddenly it all makes sense. The World Cup is big, passionate and fast. The players are playing for their country. You know who you want to win. It's genuinely exciting. If I stop Ali, stop men, watching England games, then in time I, by proxy, will have to stop watching England (and Scotland) games too. And while I could obviously live without 'friendlies', I'd miss the World Cup. Ali and I had some very enjoyable nights watching England in big tournaments; it brought us together. Gazza and Shearer; Seaman and Pearce; Rio and Becks.

But then, thinking about it, I'd always end up getting annoyed. Perhaps it's what Ali was talking about in the restaurant last week with his musings on 'hope'. You see,

I'd always hope it was going to be fair and the best team would win. It wasn't and they didn't.

The World Cup generates so much excitement, gets all that attention, inspires all that commitment (even from me!), and then the whole caboodle normally hinges on a bit of cheating or a referee completely missing an important incident that even I can see – a push, a trip, a shirt-pull, a blatant offside. And nothing is done about it!

For a start, I can't understand why they don't have more officials. It's the World Cup, surely they could afford it? Tennis – a sport normally played by just two players on a fairly small court – has nine officials. Football – on its huge pitch – has three officials for twenty-two players. By my maths, that means tennis has thirty-three times more officials per player. And tennis uses technology too. So does rugby. And cricket. Why doesn't football? I'll tell you why.

I think they could easily use technology in football, but they know that if the referee's decisions were all backed up with video analysis, if the game was fair and the better team always won, then men would have nothing to argue about at work or in the pub; the pundits would have nothing to analyse at half-time or replay over and over again after the match and before the *Ten O'Clock News*. And on the *Ten O'Clock News*.

Football fans and players, I think, like the martyrdom of it all: 'Oh, poor me! I should have scored! We should have won!'; 'Feel my pity! See my injustice! Love me more!' It fits in with the British psyche: not wanting to accept defeat; having a get-out.

No. If Ali was giving up football, he had to go the whole way. And so did I. He had to give up En-ger-land too. I rang him.

32

Bursting the Balloon

'That's Ronni; mind if I get it?' I ask my patient dresser. She nods a quiet, red-headed assent.

'Hi, Ronni. I can't talk long; I'm just in my dressing room having a load of balloons shoved down my trousers before I sing "Money Makes the World Go Round" . . .'

'I must come and see this show . . .'

'Yes, you must.'

'Anyway, I was just thinking . . . Do you remember that time when we watched England v. Argentina in France '98 and you wore your little England shirt with "McGowan" on the back . . .'

'Yes, and you swore at Beckham when he got sent off!'

'Yes, I did! And remember, Ali, when we watched England's semi-final in Euro '96 . . .?'

'Yes. And you asked me if I could get tickets if we got through to the final because Baddiel and Skinner were bound to be there, so why couldn't you and I go . . .'

'And then Southgate missed his penalty.'

'Yes. Ow!'

'What was that noise?'

'Sometimes the balloons pop.'

'Sorry,' says my patient dresser, laughing and blushing.

'And remember when we were at that dinner, Ali, on the night of England's quarter-final with Portugal in Euro 2004 . . .'

'Oh, yeah! And they had two televisions at either end of the table showing the game . . .'

'And the magician got cross with us because we shouted, "Come on, Stevie G!" during his act?'

'Yes. Ow!'

'Was that another balloon?'

'Yes, it got caught on my suspender belt.'

My patient dresser leaves, giggling and pointing at her slim watch for some reason.

'But, Ali, didn't we have some nice times watching England together . . .?'

'We did. We really did. You can't beat watching an England game – especially with someone you love.'

'I know. Well, it's got to stop.'

'Right.'

'And I know they're not in Euro 2008, but that's out too, remember. I know you can do it.'

'I'll do it if you come and see *Cabaret* . . .'

'I'll be there. Can you get me two tickets for Friday night? It's your last week, isn't it?'

'Yes. I can't believe it, but it's . . . Shit! That's my cue!'

33

The Girl in the Pub

Summer was in mid-flow. Ali's run in *Cabaret* was unexpectedly coming to an end. He would have free time on his hands for a few weeks. Now was my chance to get him to do some other things while there was no football to be watched or read about or listened to. Then, when the whole sorry business started again, I'd have armed him against it. But where should I take him? What should I do with him?

Given his addictive personality, maybe I could encourage him to become an expert on something else. If he used the time that he invested in football in other ways, Ali could become an aficionado of all sorts of subjects: history, art, politics. I mentioned this to him in the cramped Lyric pub after I'd finally seen the show . . .

'Think, Ali, of all the other things there are in life to learn about and know about, other than the history of Brighton Football Club.'

'I don't actually know that much about the history of Brighton Football Club,' says Ali. 'Other than that they play at the Withdean Stadium in Brighton, having been forced out of their home at the Goldstone Ground in Hove, and they reached the FA Cup Final in 1983, losing to Manchester United 4–0 in a replay after a 2–2 draw, and haven't played in the top division of English football since 1985 . . .'

'Well, I didn't mean literally . . .'

'Coventry City (1980–1990), on the other hand, I could tell you loads about. And Leeds United (1971–1979).'

'I was just using Brighton as an example!'

God help me!

'But think, Ali, think . . . are you listening to me?'

'Yes . . .'

'Why are you waving at that girl?'

'She waved at me.'

'Think of all the other areas of life you could be an expert on if your head wasn't full of useless old football statistics.'

'Like all the things *you're* an expert on, you mean, Ronni?'

He'd got me there. Not being a football addict I should, in theory, know more than I do about other things, but somehow life got in the way. I would love to be taken in hand and have someone sort out big reading lists and play lists for me, pushing me in all the right artistic directions, like some sort of cultural butler. But, even then, I'd never have the time. I'm always too busy making food for the children. Less a lady of letters and more a lady of lettuce.

'Well done, by the way. You were terrific . . .'

'Really? You're not just saying that?'

'I can honestly say it's the best thing I've ever seen you do . . . in a camp German accent while wearing leather shorts and knee-length boots.'

Ali certainly didn't look or sing like an average football fan in that show.

'It's going to be odd without it.'

'I'll keep you busy. I've got all sorts of things lined up for you . . .'

'That sounds ominous.'

'Keep next Monday free for a start. You're going out!'

'Where?'

'You'll see soon enough,' I said, enigmatically – and to cover the fact that I hadn't worked it out yet. 'But you think about what you'd like to do too, will you, Ali?'

'Yes.'

'Promise?'

'Promise.'

'Cross your heart and . . .'

'Why's that girl waving at me again, Ronni?'

'Probably because you're the only vaguely attractive, straight man in here who's not watching the football on the giant screens.'

'It's Euro 2008.'

'You see the benefits now?'

'Ummm . . .'

'Either that, Ali, or she's trying to tell you that you've forgotten to take your eye make-up off.'

'Oh! I'm always doing that.'

'I think you like it!'

'Shut up!'

'Or *she* does . . .'

34

Kicking and Screaming

Step Fourteen: Take Him to Cultural Events

Ali was doing so, so well; he'd seemed really happy about everything in the pub the other night – apart from the fact that his show was coming off and he had no other work lined up for the foreseeable future. I was doing a good thing. I'd known it all along really. I started to feel like I was giving him a total character make-over. I felt like Gok Wan – without the glasses, obviously. Or the tan. Or a penis.

So where was I going to take him? The choice was vital. I said I'd got lots of things lined up for him. Well, I did have lots of options but I had to choose one. And if there's one thing I'm really bad at, it's making choices.

OPERA?

The best thing about opera is the going. I don't mean the journey, obviously; I mean the pomp, the gilt and the grandeur of it all. And how it makes you feel cultured and gives you a lovely warm feeling of general smugness. But, it has to be said, it is one of those many things in life that I feel I should enjoy more than I do. A bit like visiting ruins. I know it's good for me but I don't necessarily enjoy it. It's like a sort of cultural cough medicine.

Even if I did find an opera Ali liked, opera couldn't

really replace football in his life; it's a one-off treat and it's all far too formal. A bloke can hardly kick off his shoes and put his feet up on the seat in front while he drinks a can of beer, tucks into his Indian takeaway and shouts obscenities at the singers, can he?

'Come on! Keep away from the wings, you wanker! Go centre stage!' Although if that sort of behaviour was, in fact, de rigueur at the opera, I'm sure we'd see a huge surge in its popularity among men.

Years ago, Alistair and I went to see *A Midsummer Marriage* by Benjamin Britten at the ENO. We'd been avidly watching a documentary series about the company on BBC One and both said we'd not seen enough opera in our lives and that neither of us had ever been to the ENO. So we got some very expensive tickets – and went.

It was one of those strangely out-of-context operas where they were all singing in major, grand operatic mode, but in a seemingly discordant way. It was difficult music and all done in modern dress: everyone was skipping around with shorts and T-shirts on, sitting on blankets and carrying picnic baskets. It was like a highbrow Maltesers advert.

Alistair, I seem to remember, was very fidgety and frustrated by it all. Well, we both were. It was in three acts; we left after two.

On asking Ali for his critique, he said he hadn't cared for the music but he liked the shorts because it made him think for a second that he was at a football match.

I've been back to the opera since and enjoyed it, but taking Ali again would be too much of a risk and would just send him running back to football, I was sure.

OPERA

If Ronni were to take me to the opera, I'd love it. I ought to go more often. Why do I always say that about the arts, 'I ought to go more often'? Maybe because deep down I know I'm wasting too much time watching football.

Maybe I'm still too young for opera, though. Most people don't get into it until they're sixty. I don't know why. It is just one of those things you often come to later in life – like Catholicism, port and crystallised ginger. And girls with big bottoms. But Ronni always said I was old before my time. Maybe she'll take me to the opera.

THE BALLET?

I need to take him somewhere new, exciting and dynamic. The ballet! I don't think Ali's ever been to the ballet – he'll love it! I'm prejudiced because I love ballet and, like countless other women, did ballet when I was a little girl.

Just as Alistair can wax lyrical about the smells and sounds of his early football experiences, I can still vividly recollect the sweet, musty smell of Mrs Mitchell's ballet class – and, indeed, of Mrs Mitchell. And my love is no less valid: it has the same link to childhood hopes and dreams and innocence. The difference is that you won't find me screaming obscenities when a principal dancer's *entrechat* doesn't meet my expectations, and I don't need to check the attendance at every ballet nationwide.

On reflection, this might be less to do with me being more well-balanced mentally than your average football fan and more to do with me being in denial that I could never have been a professional dancer. For a start, I was the wrong shape – too tall and nowhere near delicate enough. I was more rustic-peasant-built-for-potato-picking than ethereal-fairy-princess-built-for-*jetés*-and-being-picked-up-by-powdery-men-in-vests. Most ballet dancers have such petite frames that you wonder where their internal organs go. Certainly not side by side. Perhaps they have some sort of rota system:

RIGHT-HAND KIDNEY: Oi, Liver! Budge up! You're in my space! I thought we agreed, Monday to Wednesday *I'm* here.
LIVER: It's not my fault, Kidney; I've got that bloody pancreas up my arse!
PANCREAS: I don't know what you're complaining about, Liver. You've got plenty of room; you're next to her stomach.
STOMACH: What are you saying, Pancreas? That I don't do anything? I'll have you know I've had to process a whole olive and a sip of mineral water today!

Thirdly, there was the fact that I have a wonky pelvis. But not in an erotic, alluring way like Shakira but in a sad, pathological way like Quasimodo.

And finally, and this is the real bummer, I couldn't have been a professional ballet dancer because . . . I was crap. Not good enough. Nowhere near. Never was. But, rather pathetically, I worship dancers; I love being around them. And if you are ever around dancers, particularly in a bar, beware! They are hazardous! They're so supple that their legs can just spring out and kick your drink into your face – or, worse still, into someone else's face.

Which brings me back to thinking that Alistair, or any football fan for that matter, might enjoy ballet – there is kicking involved. What's more, dancers, like footballers, are at the peak of fitness. It's athletic and it's fast-moving.

I give Ali a call . . .

'How about a trip to the ballet?'

There's silence at the other end.

I persevere. 'I think you might really like it because it's similar to football in many ways.'

'In what ways would that be, Ronni? Perhaps in the way that the forest fairy has to get back to her floaty lair before the simple woodcutter sees her and snitches on her to the witch.'

'You know, you're horribly cynical sometimes. That's what football has done to you.'

'Well, I just don't know how you can like ballet so much.'

'Because I have an empathy with it. I was going to be a dancer, you know.'

'Oh, *were* you?'

'Yes. The only reason I'm not is because of my pelvis. My husband says I'm "rotated".'

'Yeah, not far enough from him.'

'Ali!'

'I thought the only reason you weren't a ballet dancer is because you were terrible at it . . .'

'There was that too.'

'Anyway, you only like ballet because it's full of goblins and talking swans and magical creatures.'

It always comes down to this: Ali thinks that I live in my own little world. That I am a fantasist! Me, of all people! He's just jealous because he has never seen a troll ride a unicorn side-saddle.

I'll give up on the ballet. I'll call him back when I think of something else.

'I'll call you back when I think of something else.'

'Call me back when you think of something else.'

'I will. Are you being sar-carstic, Ali?'

'No.'

BALLET

I've never liked the ballet. Just before I fell for Ronni, I went on a date to Sadler's Wells with a beautiful Scottish woman with huge eyes and hair the colour of a Caramac.

'Do you like dance?' she asked.

'Yes', I said, because I liked her more.

So we sat at Sadler's Wells watching the ballet. In fact, there were two ballets – one in each half. I had a programme on my knee. I can't remember the name of the other ballet but the second one listed was *Thérèse Raquin*. This was better news. I'd only just read the book and loved it. It was unforgettable, with the most vivid descriptions of lust and murder. I struggled and frowned my way through the first ballet wondering what the hell I was going to say about it with my pathetically small dance vocabulary, and decided that simple honesty would be best. My doe-eyed friend turned to me in the interval and said, 'What did you think?'

'Well', I said, 'I have to say I'm looking forward to the second one a lot more because I didn't really get much from that and I love *Thérèse Raquin*.'

'That was *Thérèse Raquin*', she said. Date over.

MUSIC?

Music! I could take him to a gig! After all, there are many similarities between going to see a live-music gig and going to a football match: the overcrowding, the warm beer and the anti-social behaviour for starters. The thing is, he's just not that into music.

MUSIC

I love music. Well, I love certain music. But I am fussy, and I do have a bit of a problem with live music. Basically, because I only have music on at home while I'm doing something else (I've never been one for having a Walkman or iPods – I like listening to the world too much), I always associate music with doing other things. So, if I ever go to see live music, I always want to iron or clean or read. And I never know what to wear.

I like the idea of hearing music performed live. And I've been to gigs. Well, about three. I also got asked to go to recordings of Jools Holland's *Later* a couple of times. I agonised about what to wear and, in case there were cut-away shots of me, I sat trying to look cool and like I was enjoying it at the same time. I ended up looking like I needed the toilet. But it might be fun to get into the whole music 'scene', as long as Ronni told me what to wear – and they let me take in a duster, an iron and a book.

CAFES?

Perhaps I could just get him to sit in cafes, looking myste-rious and French. He'd like that; he loves everything

French. Although when I was going out with Alistair, he would never want to go the local cafe for breakfast or even for a coffee as he thought it was 'a waste of time'.

This is true to a point. I mean, if you are on the frontline of a disaster zone and, instead of helping the wounded, the suffering or the desperate, you nip down to the nearest watering hole for an espresso, then, yes, it would be deemed a waste of time. But why is spending a few minutes chatting with your nearest and dearest over a few arabica beans considered a waste of time compared to spending hours at home every morning staring at the football results?!

CAFES

I hope she doesn't start taking me to cafes. She used to do that. I could never understand why she wanted to go out and buy an overpriced coffee ten metres from the house when she could have made one at home for nothing. Ah, no! I think I'm safe. We won't go to cafes because she knows they all have newspapers in them nowadays, and we know what newspapers have all over the back pages – temptation!

NIGHTCLUBS?

For me, nightclubs are located in some dim and distant, pre-children and pre-responsibility era, in the days before I had to be up every morning at 5.30 a.m. with bright, hyper toddlers brightly picking up bits of brightly coloured plastic. Nowadays, my idea of the perfect night out is 'a night in' – and being asleep by ten. Oh, the hedonism of it!

Anyway, going to a nightclub doesn't sound like even a

moderately good night out: being deafened by music, unable to talk to anyone and stepping over vomit in the toilets – I can get all that from drop-in toddler groups. And, if I'm honest, even in my pre-children and pre-responsibility era, I still found nightclubs disappointing. And intimidating. I think it was the fact that there was someone standing at the door of the establishment waiting to reject me on the grounds that I wasn't young, gorgeous or cool enough. The irony is, of course, that you're in much more need of a good night out if you are not young, gorgeous or cool – in order to cheer yourself up.

Needless to say, Alistair isn't good with nightclubs either. Actually, when we were going out together, we complemented each other rather well. He was organised; I was disorganised. He was cautious; I was spontaneous. He was a man; I was a woman. But what we both had in common was that we were not cool.

I was always uncool – even when I was young, much to my dismay. Yes, I looked like a Goth, but it wasn't intentional; I was just very pale and very dark-haired, and tended to wear dark colours as I was always worried about my weight.

People who are born cool fascinate me. I don't understand how they do it. In my superficial way, I would rank people who can tie a scarf in a stylish way well above some brilliant scholar. I am in awe of 'cool'. I think it stems from my primary-school days. I longed to be one of those tidy little girls whose tights always stayed up. I wore the same tights as everyone else, but my tights were permanently falling down. Consequently, I waddled around with a perpetual web between my blue woollen legs, like a strange duck.

When I see people now who are the same age that Alistair and I were when we first met, they seem so young and free, yet I didn't really feel that at the time. Probably because Ali and I didn't do the sort of things that young people do. Alistair was so self-contained and controlled. It drove me mad. He didn't like clubs or loud music or dancing or drinking or fast cars or fast anything. He just hated the thought of being out of control in any way. Consequently, there was an element of me that was slightly relieved that he liked something so normal, so male as football. It took the edge off his retentive streak, brought out his passion and his anger and made him less of an old fogey. Oh, no! Have I discovered another 'plus' for football? No, it's done him more harm than good. It did me more harm than good. And I've nearly, finally, got it out of his system.

NIGHTCLUBS

Maybe she'll take me clubbing. That might be fun – apart from the fact that I don't like loud music. Or being out of control. Or seeing people out of control. And the one thing I've never done to music is dance. I love dancing on stage but just idly moving from side to side has never done anything for me. It always reminds me of being in old people's homes.

ART?

So opera, ballet, live-music gigs and nightclubs are out then. Where can I take him? There must be something . . .

What do I know most about? Art! I know about art; I can help open it up to him. A whole new wonderful world! If I could get the boys at Holloway interested in art, surely I can do the same for Ali. It'll be tough; men and women never have a good time at an art gallery together unless they are in a Woody Allen film. But I believe in Ali now. Yes, I'll take him to an art gallery!

ART

God, I hope she doesn't take me to an art gallery . . .

35

The Art Gallery

'You'll really enjoy it, Ali. Stop behaving like a child!'

'Well, you're behaving like a teacher!'

'I'm not.'

'Are.'

'I'm not. And pick your feet up when you walk. You'll ruin your shoes!'

The National Gallery houses one of the finest collections of Western European art in the world. There was bound to be something there that got Ali excited. I hoped there would be; it was years since I'd been. I probably should have done a recce and had an exact plan of what to show Ali to meet his exacting tastes, but we had a good few hours and the National Gallery never changes that much. It would be perfect – and it was free. Which was fortunate, as I was paying.

To soften the blow, and as it was a bright sunny day, I'd suggested we meet in Hyde Park and walk up to Trafalgar Square. That was my first mistake.

'Why didn't we just meet there?' he grumps.

'I thought you might like a little walk. I could tell you a little bit about what you're going to see. And you get to see a bit of sunshine. You like sunshine, don't you?'

'I like *sitting* in it. God, look at all this litter!'

'Ali, will you cheer up, please?'

'Well, I'm really not happy about this.'

'You're going to an art gallery, not to death row. Just give it a go!'

'I hate art,' he mumbles, like a surly teenager.

'You can't say you hate art.'

'But I do.'

'Listen, Ali!' I said, stopping dead in the middle of the park. 'If you don't cheer up and try and enjoy yourself, do you know what I'm going to do?'

'What?'

'I'm going to pull your pants down in front of all these people and smack your bottom. Is that what you want?'

'No.'

'Well, that's what's going to happen. Now cheer up! I went to a football match with you, didn't I?'

'Yes.'

'Two, in fact.'

'Yes.'

'Right. Now, let's try and . . .'

'Why's that man staring?'

'Because he probably heard me say I was going to pull your pants down if you don't cheer up!'

'Shhh!'

'Well, then. Behave! Stop your nonsense!'

'Is this what you're like with your children?'

'No. D'you know why?'

'Why?'

'Because they're willing to try new things. They're not stuck in their ways like you. They're always inquisitive!'

'That's because you've never taken them to an art gallery.'

'Ali, I've given up my afternoon to do this with you – *for* you. Now cheer up and apply yourself, or you'll get nothing from it and you'll have wasted both our times.'

'That's not strictly grammatical.'

'It doesn't matter! Life's not all about language! That's why this will be good for you. No words. No football.'

'No fun.'

'What?'

'Nothing.'

We walked on in silence for a bit and then my phone went. It was my agent, saying the lovely people from *QI* wanted me to go on the show again. This was great news! Not only did I love doing the show but her call had broken the tension between me and Ali.

As I got the details from her, I noticed out of the corner of my eye that Ali was cheering up. About time! My well-chosen, if ungrammatical, words had obviously worked on him. Then I realised that he was smiling because of all the beautiful tanned women wandering through the sunshine in their spaghetti-strap tops and ballet pumps. He was checking them out from behind his sunglasses. And they were giving him some very coy glances back. I needed to take his mind off that.

'So, Ali,' I said, struggling to put my phone back in my bag, 'let's get to the root of this. Why don't you like art?'

'I don't know. I suppose I never painted, so I don't appreciate the skill involved.'

'You never painted?'

'No.'

'Everyone paints when they're a child. Kids love it! My two were having so much fun this morning.'

'Is that why you've got paint up your arm?'

'Oh! Yes. Why didn't you tell me?'

'I thought it was a bruise at first and didn't want to say anything in case . . .'

'Wipe it off!'

Ali took out his handkerchief and spat on it like a grand-mother.

'No! Not like that. Oh, it doesn't matter.'

'Don't worry. You'll look artistic. All the little students at the gallery will be thinking, "Wow! Look at her. She's like a real artist, man!"'

'That's hardly why people go to art galleries, Ali. They go there to look at the work of real geniuses. To be moved, inspired, impressed.'

'Like football then.'

I count to ten. Well, four.

'I can't believe you never painted.'

'I was hopeless at it.'

Ah! That was it! Ali never liked doing anything he wasn't instantly good at. It was his vanity again.

'Well, I mean, I used to draw a bit when I was younger.'

'What did you draw?'

'Football scenes . . .'

I should have known

'. . . and Tom and Jerry.'

'Really?'

'Yes. At my uncle's house. We stayed over and there was nothing to do. So he suggested I draw something. "What?" I said. "What about Tom and Jerry?" he said, because I loved the cartoons. So I drew them. And afterwards he said, "So, which is which?"'

'How old were you?'

'Twenty-six.'

'What?!'

'No! Eight. Or something.'

'Here it is. The National Gallery. Prepare, Ali, to be impressed!'

We head off to look at some old Dutch Masters. The only old Dutch Masters who had ever been of any note to Alistair to date were Ruud Gullit and Dennis Bergkamp, so this would be an education for him. Rather than bombard him with facts – and because I'd never been too 'up' on the Dutch Masters – I let Ali wander around by himself and soak it all in. I watch him, hoping to see some appreciative nods, some analysis of the brushstrokes. But he just stares blankly at the pictures, obviously incredulous that Rembrandt could have wasted so much time painting a square of satin in so much detail, when he could have been watching *Football Focus*.

'Isn't he a genius, Ali? He brought such emotional and psychological depth to his portraits.'

'I find them a bit gloomy, to be honest,' he says – this from a man whose idea of 'uplifting' is watching Mark Lawrenson moaning about poor defending.

'This is what men did in the seventeenth century. Before silly football! I mean, think, Ali, just think how much more wonderful art and music and drama might have been created if men hadn't been too busy watching Derby play Coventry on Sky Sports 1.'

'That's a Championship game; it would be on Sky Sports 2.'

I clearly have a lot of work still to do.

We move on to the Impressionists room. I figure just the name might pique Ali's interest – that and the fact that they were French. Surely I can't lose in here!

'Notice the emphasis on light, the way the artist brilliantly captures all its changing qualities, and the beautiful open composition, the visible, bold brushstrokes,' I say, as we study Monet's *The Beach at Trouville*.

'I'm sure it's very pretty, but they're all a bit chocolate boxy for me, really, Ronni, these. A bit twee and crowd-pleasing.'

'What are you saying? This group of artists were the radicals of their time! They were cutting edge! At first, they were derided by the people, and their work was totally rejected by the establishment, and it was only because of a salon set up by . . .'

Ali has suddenly wandered off and is gazing at a painting by Degas of a naked woman doing her ablutions.

'I like this one,' he says, peering closely at the woman's breasts. 'She needs to get her cellulite sorted out, though.'

'Ali! That's just the way they used paint. Honestly! Now, listen, you keep looking around; I've got to go to the loo. I'll be back in a jiffy. And no running off!'

When I get back from the Ladies, Ali has struck up a conversation with a pretty young redhead and another slightly older lady. He's waving his arms around expressively and looking at the floor, smirking after everything he says – a sure sign of him flirting! I hover by a Pissarro and listen.

'No, she's not my sister, she's my mum!'

'Oh, that's very sweet of you though. What a charmer! Isn't he a charmer, Emily?'

'So, what brings you girls down from Nottingham?'

'How did you know we were from Nottingham?'

'It's kinda my job! Accents and everything.'

'Oh, how wonderful! Well, I came down to visit Emily. She's just split up from her boyfriend, you see, and . . .'

'Mum . . .!'

'Well, she has. You have. She has. And she wanted some company. And my husband's busy with his football summer school, so . . .'

'Oh, football!' says Ali. 'Doesn't it just take over men's lives?'

Was I hearing properly?

'Oh, yes! My boyfriend is . . . well, my ex-boyfriend was always watching it. I just don't get it. It's so boring!'

'Isn't it?' said Ali. 'I really don't know what men see in it. I've never understood it. I never "got on the football train", so to speak.'

What???

'Oh, how refreshing! Isn't that refreshing, Emily, to hear a man say that?'

'Yes, Mum. It's refreshing.'

'So refreshing.'

And on he went . . .

'I honestly like nothing better than spending time in art galleries . . . and museums – especially on hot sunny days. It's so nice to spurn the beckoning sun and just journey inside into the cool recesses of a gallery and into the dark corners of our own souls. Don't you find?'

Unbelievable! By getting in touch with his feminine side, he was clearly hoping to get in touch with Emily's feminine side – and back – and front.

As the smirking and flirting went on, it suddenly dawned on me. Banning him from football was making him more interested in girls! And, as he was no longer interested in football, they were more interested in him!! First, there was the girl at the pub and now Emily.

This was either potentially a great weapon in my fight against football or a terrible 'own goal' on my part. For a second, I felt like Oppenheimer. What had I done? I could accidentally annihilate swathes of relationships that I'd intended to improve!

I extract Ali from the clutches of Emily and Emily's mother – who could also have been within his sights, I wasn't sure (forty-three is an odd age for a man – like property values, he can go up as well as down) – by pretending to be Ali's girlfriend or by barking like a dog. I can't quite remember which.

We continue on our tour into the Pre-Raphaelites room and, for what it was worth, I give Ali some more pearls of art wisdom.

'Notice the fidelity to nature and the vivid, realistic colour. This was considered typical of Italian painting before Raphael – hence the name, "Pre-Raphaelites".'

'Say that again?'

'Notice the fidelity to nature and the vivid, realistic colour. This was . . . you just want me to say this so you can impress Emily, don't you?'

'No! I'm genuinely interested in the art! It's amazing!'

'Forget it, Ali! Just forget it! I can't believe this! All the time I've given up for you and it comes down to this. Sex! Well, fuck you, Ali! Fuck you!'

'Ronni! Don't be . . .'

'I'm going home!'

'Ronni!'

I don't normally look back but something that day made me turn round. And as I turned my head to look at Ali's lost, beaky little face, I saw Emily's mum pressing a folded piece of lined paper into his hand. It could only mean one thing: her daughter's number.

ALISTAIR: The art gallery was surprisingly good fun. I may even go again. With Emily.

36

No Escape!

Three days after the disaster in the art gallery, I go to Sardinia with my family. It feels good to be getting away from the whole programme for a while. From football. Having said that, while going on holiday means you get away from a lot of annoying things in your life, it doesn't always guarantee a break from football. Far from it, in fact.

I only took one exotic, faraway holiday with Alistair in our years together. In 1995, after months of nagging, I got him to agree to go somewhere further than his beloved France. Belgium it was, then. But, the year after, I pulled off the amazing feat of getting him on a plane to Mauritius. I was so excited. I had never gone long haul before, never had the 'paradise' experience. I'd never seen white sand – or a coconut on anything other than a stall at a fair. All my family holidays were spent either in a caravan in Herne Bay or, if we were feeling flush, a trip up the Manchester Ship Canal. Alistair and I both agreed that not having had exotic holidays as children made us appreciate our trip to Mauritius even more. It made us feel we'd earned it. We'd arrived!

Our hotel was beautiful, right on the white sandy beach, and the weather was lovely . . . for that first afternoon. The next day it rained. And the next day. And the next. Then, for a change, it didn't rain . . . it poured. But the next day it stopped pouring . . . and developed into torrential monsoon-like flooding which lasted for the entire ten days we were there.

So much for me finally, for once in my life getting anything approaching a tan. So much for the heaps of books we were going to read in the sun. So much for the nights of endless . . . Well, anyway, our plans changed. Our horizons narrowed. In fact, one day, they completely disappeared, so heavy was the rain.

So there I was on my dream holiday with a man whose concept of hedonism is having an extra sugar in his tea (so even drowning my disappointment in a mutual bloodbath of cocktails was out), reduced to taking a variety of coach trips to explore the island. We may as well have gone to the Isle of Wight.

If you've been to Mauritius you'll know there is nothing to explore. It's all lovely, long beaches and vast, green sugar-beet plantations. We sat on steamed-up coaches, day after day, along with several honeymooning couples, who, due to the colossal disappointment of the bad weather, were already at each other hammer and tongs.

We were on a sightseeing trip but couldn't see any of the sights. The windows were steamed up with disappointment and the breath of angry words; the rain was coming down through the mist outside. It was like travelling round the island inside a party balloon. I thought things had reached their lowest ebb when we got out at the cafe which was billed as the island's highest point – 'with breathtaking views' – and were unable to see further than the wet metal chair leg in front of us.

That, however, was before we got to the town of Curepipe – a disappointing place, full of ugliness and oil and shops that had neither charm nor swank. It was a bit like the indoor market in Accrington. And then, to make things even worse, in a corner of a covered arcade was a shop devoted to football. To English football. And to Manchester United. In Mauritius. In the middle of the Indian Ocean. In the middle of my dream holiday. So far from home and so near to home. I couldn't believe it. Man United shirts, scarves, posters, pennants and flags. Even here, the spectre of football, British football, red in shirt and claw, was staring me in the face. It was like seeing the poor dead little girl in *Don't Look Now* – a flash of an old, sad, red reality from another world, another time. Had we really seen it? Yes. There it was – squat and ugly and English. I wanted to cry; Alistair wanted a picture. There was no escape from it.

They say that one day man will be able to travel to the moon or to Mars with Richard Branson (personally speaking, if he could design a decent train for his Virgin network, with luggage racks that are big enough for something thicker than a music case with nothing in it but 'Für Elise' and windows that are actually next to your face and not next to the back of your seat, I'd be more impressed). But I guarantee that even if you can holiday on a different planet in the not too distant future, and if the aliens that live there are friendly, the first thing they'll ask as we step off Branson's rocket will be, 'Did you see that Man United game yesterday? This Chilean guy is the new Wayne Rooney, innit?'

37

Elland Road Revisited – 'Suitgate'

After the sad early end of *Cabaret*, I took a rare holiday. I had been offered a new job playing one of the two leads in *They're Playing Our Song* – a rather corny old 1980s musical play – opposite Connie Fisher at The Chocolate Factory (a thriving small theatre in Southwark). I needed a rest before I began; it was now or never. I've never been a big traveller. So I took the train to the South of France, stayed in a beautiful hotel just outside Cannes and didn't move from my spot by the pool for a week.

I was happy to go alone. I was tired and I fancied some reading time. I had thought briefly of taking Emily but knew, even if she'd said yes, that that would have been a different sort of holiday. I needed no stress. I could come back to her. And, nice though she was, she liked art galleries!

I sat by the pool, in the sun, watching the stylish French walk past from behind my sunglasses. Even the waiters are stylish here and look to have a pride in themselves and their job. God, I love France! Even their cemeteries are to die for! And no one pulls off a white jacket like a French waiter. A white jacket . . . As I lay in the French heat, half asleep, half awake, half dreaming, half remembering, I suddenly saw myself in my mind's eye . . .

I was smiling from ear to ear.

'You look happy, baby. Who was that?' said Ronni,

walking into the green study in our old house in Clapham in 1998.

I'd had a phone call from someone called Jason Madeley. I recognised the surname. Ronni didn't. Paul Madeley had been one of my boyhood heroes – one of Don Revie's 'family'. One of my family. I'd had his picture on my bedroom wall.

Jason Madeley had asked me if I would be willing to perform at the Leeds United Player of the Year dinner on May 5th 1998 at Elland Road. I didn't need to think twice.

'By the way, I presume your father was . . .'

'Paul Madeley, yes.'

'You do know I had his picture on my bedroom wall when I was seven?' I could have said sixteen but decided to temper it a little bit.

'Were you a Leeds fan then?' he asked in his light Leeds accent.

'Yes, isn't that why you asked me?'

'No. I asked you because Andy Gray said you're good.'

'Right. Thanks. See you in May, then.'

Some gigs loom in the diary. Some gigs throb. This gig was off the scale. But I was never nervous; I knew I'd be all right at Elland Road.

I've never been one for dinner suits, all that 'black-tie' nonsense. If it said 'Black Tie' on an invitation, my heart used to sink. I'd never looked good in one. Above all else, with a dinner jacket, your shirt collar has to be well fitting, and I have a very small neck. Ronni used to gently tease me about it. In fact, she unintentionally gave me a complex about it which exists to this day. But I would still always wear a dinner suit when I was speaking at a black-tie event. That is, until one of the bookers once said to me,

'Oh, you can wear what you want. You're the entertainer; you don't count!'

And so I did. And I'd never been picked up on it. For 'black-tie' events I wore an ordinary black suit with an open-necked shirt. Or, if my agent told me it was a 'lounge-suit' affair, I wore a lounge suit but with the tie undone so it wasn't tight around my 'tiny' neck.

May 5th 1998 was a warm day. As I'd been told by my agent that this was a 'lounge-suit' affair, I set off for Leeds (for the first time since leaving university), travelling light in a cream, linen suit. Arriving at Elland Road, I was full of anticipation. I stood in the foyer of the main stand, looking at the framed photographs on the walls of former players, former glories: Lee Chapman celebrating a goal in 1992; Allan Clarke, Paul Madeley, Billy Bremner, Peter Lorimer and my dad's favourite, Norman 'Bite Yer Legs' Hunter, holding aloft the FA Cup in 1972 and the League Championship in 1974. Memories . . .

I saw some of the current Leeds players, who nodded at me one by one as I arrived, frowning slightly and whispering to each other. They looked immaculate, fit and wore too much hair gel. And they were all wearing dinner suits. Dinner suits and bow ties.

Then, Paul Madeley's son, Jason, made himself known to me and introduced the Leeds United manager, the sober and dour former Arsenal boss George Graham.

George was an imposing man with steely eyes and a sharp Scottish accent that could slice cheese. He had become known as a strict disciplinarian: you didn't want to mess with George Graham. He had, strangely, been involved in (and scored in) the first English football match I'd ever seen on television – the 1971 FA Cup Final between Liverpool and Arsenal. And there he was, standing before me twenty-seven years later, welcoming me to Leeds United Football Club.

'Nice to meet you, son. I hear very good things' – obviously, he didn't remember the Arsenal gig of '93.

'Do you need somewhere to change, son?' he asked.

'This is all I've got with me; I hope it's okay.'

'It's not. Where's your dinner suit?'

'I . . . er . . . my agent . . . I thought it was a lounge-suit do.'

'Black tie, son. You can't perform in that.'

He had a small army of people with mobile phones and walkie-talkies around him, including Jason Madeley.

'What time does Moss Bros close, Jason?'

'Six o'clock, I think, Mr Graham,' said Jason Madeley.

'Is there not one on the Headrow that's open late?'

'I think there's one in York that's open late.'

'York?! Fucking York! What about the Headrow?'

'I don't think it is.'

'Don't *think* it is?'

'But I can look into it if . . .'

'Look into it. He can't perform in that. You can't perform in that, son.'

George was then suddenly surrounded by lots of women with pale backs in sparkling frocks, and well-to-do northern businessmen with particularly thick necks. For several minutes, I was forgotten – and so was my predicament.

I was held to one side by Jason Madeley and the men with the walkie-talkies, who were talking to anyone who would listen about Moss Bros' opening hours and whether there was a branch open within a ten-mile radius. Jason

Madeley smiled, pursing his lips in that what-can-you-do? sort of way. It wasn't looking good.

I was on the threshold of Elland Road, about to finally make my Leeds debut – was I to be denied because of a stupid Ronni Ancona-induced, thin neck-based moment of sartorial stupidity? My bloody agent! Why, of all times, did it have to be tonight that the wires had got crossed?

I could see more of the players arriving, some of them looking at me and frowning, shaking their famous heads at my blunder. A cream suit!

Leeds wear white – surely that might count for something?

'What's the news?' Suddenly George Graham was back at my side again.

'Can't get anything from Moss Bros, Mr Graham, they're all closed,' said Jason Madeley.

'Well, you can't perform in that son. "Black tie" means "Black tie". You'll not look good. And if you don't look good, I don't look good. What size are you?'

'Forty chest, thirty-three inside leg and . . .' Why was George Graham asking my measurements?

'Shoes?'

'Forty-five.'

'What?'

'Eleven.'

'No. That's no good. I was going to send home for a spare suit from my wardrobe but you're bigger than me all over. Bloody hell!'

Suddenly, out of the corner of my eye, I saw a familiar face. It was a greyer face, and the man who was 6ft 1 in 1972 was a little more stooped than he had been on my bedroom wall. But it was him: Paul Madeley's defensive colleague, the most feared central defender in Europe in the early 1970s, the man they nicknamed 'Bite Yer Legs', my old university friend Andrew Sherlock's landlord, my dad's favourite, former Leeds United and England number 6 and guest of honour for the night . . . Norman Hunter.

And Norman was wearing a white suit! Not even cream – white!

Suddenly, he was shaking hands with his old adversary, George Graham. George, looking incredulous, introduced me to Norman Hunter, who shook my hand and said in a surprisingly high north-east accent (born, Eighton Banks), 'I hope you're going to do him tonight!' nodding mischievously at George Graham.

George flicked his head in the direction of the brightly carpeted stairs and, like a bouncer outside a nightclub, said reluctantly, 'You'd better go in, son.'

The gig went well enough, although I remember the short speech from Leeds United's Player of the Year 1998, the Norwegian Alf-Inge Haaland, actually got the biggest laughs of the night. But I can't have been too bad as I was asked back . . .

I soaked up the French sun. The lovely sun. Football was out of my life now, but I still had the memories and the connections. The memories. Unless Ronni was reading *1984*, she didn't know how to stop me *thinking* about football, did she? Did she??

I ordered a sparkling water from the white-jacketed waiter (checking to see that it wasn't going to be Badoit) and closed my eyes again. Red dots and squiggles danced against my red lids every time I blinked, like microbes on a slide. What were those dots? Were they good or bad? And again, my thoughts drifted back to football as the sun beat down. The sun . . . the sun . . . the son.

Eighteen months after the Player of the Year gig, I was on my way to Leeds again, courtesy of Jason Madeley. He'd rung the house. Would I like two tickets to see Leeds play any time? Hospitality treatment, first-class train travel, the works. I knew I wouldn't be seeing my Leeds playing but I was definitely going to go – and there was only one person I was going to take.

I rang my dad. He didn't get about much; he didn't see well these days. But he would love to come to Elland Road.

'In a box, eh, Al? Bloody hell! Who'd have thought all those years ago how much you wanted me to take you . . . and now they're asking us to go. Bloody hell!'

'I've got to do a little speech after the match in the players' lounge, but otherwise we can just watch the match.'

'I wonder if we'll meet any of the old lot . . .'

'I doubt it, Dad, but still . . . Good, eh?'

One man I knew we wouldn't meet that day would be Billy Bremner. Billy had died two years previously, but I had had the good fortune to meet him one bizarre night in Edinburgh.

I'd been asked to speak at a testimonial dinner for a Hibs player called Gordon Hunter. In truth, I didn't know much about Gordon Hunter, but when I heard that the other speaker at his testimonial dinner would be Billy Bremner nothing was going to keep me away. Billy was quite frail by that time, but he made a great speech that night. He offended most people in the room at some point, but told some wonderful stories and told them brilliantly. Here was an insight into my heroes, Don Revie's Leeds United, from the horse's mouth!

After the gig, we took a taxi back to the hotel together. Me and Billy Bremner. As we drew up at our unusually tiny hotel, Billy said to me, 'Are you going to have a drink, Alistair, son?'

'No thanks, Billy.' I knew the bar would be packed full of people and I'd not get near the wee man. 'I'm not a drinker and I think I'll go up to my bed.'

'That's a good idea. Very sensible. Maybe I'll do the same. Aye. Or we could just have a Coke or something, eh?'

'Okay. That would be nice. Thanks, Billy,' I said, my hero-worship getting the better of me.

'Good lad. Two Cokes, eh? That'll be good for me. And well done tonight. You're a funny kid.'

As we got out of the cab, we were immediately pounced on by the hotel guests, many of whom had been at the dinner.

'Hey, Billy!'

'It's Billy Bremner!'

'Away to fuck!'

'It is! It's Billy Bremner!'

'Hey, Billy!'

'Billy!'

'Billy!'

'What'll you have to drink, Billy?'

Billy looked at me. I looked at Billy. He knew what he had to do – give them what they wanted.

'A whisky, lad. Aye, a whisky.'

'One large whisky for Billy fucking Bremner!'

They surrounded him, patting him on the back, and led him into the tiny hotel. I watched him go, swallowed up in the backdraught of his own fame, and went to bed. A year later, he was dead.

So, twenty-five years on from our trip to see Leeds United play for the first time together, my dad and I see them play for the last time together.

Dad loves the train up there – 'First class!' – and can't get over the at-seat tea and coffee service. And can't resist putting the sugar sachets in his jacket pocket. What happens to people when they get over seventy? Why do they all have to steal sugar sachets from cafes, restaurants and trains?

Dad loves the ground and he really loves the executive box. We meet Jason Madeley and the chairman, Peter Ridsdale. Just before the match we meet Alf-Inge Haaland. He's injured but watches the match in the box with us and comes over with a match programme. He asks me to sign it. In front of my father, I sign the programme of a Leeds United player.

Leeds beat Bradford City 2–0, and then we go through to the Players' Lounge. There is tea and sandwiches. Dad can't believe this is free too and piles his plate high, while slyly putting yet more sugar sachets in his bulging top pocket.

I do my short comedy spot and then I can relax too. I go back to find my dad and, as I join him, it's not the players from today's game who join us. Coming towards us out of the overlit blur of static carpets and steel chairs are Paul Madeley, Allan Clarke and Norman Hunter.

'We just wanted to say hello,' says Paul Madeley.

'We love the TV show,' says Norman Hunter.

'Isn't the girl brilliant, eh? Isn't she brilliant, Norman?' says Allan Clarke.

'Very good,' says Norman Hunter.

'And beautiful,' says Allan Clarke.

'Great clavicles . . .' I say.

'Yes . . .' says Norman Hunter, frowning.

'Where did you find her?' says Allan Clarke.

'On a boat on the Thames!' says my dad.

'Well, actually . . .'

Allan Clarke pokes me regularly as we continue to talk: it's almost rude – but it's Allan Clarke! Norman Hunter is laughing with my dad, who can't resist calling him 'Bite Yer Legs' Hunter, and Paul Madeley is standing watching over us all. They're all older and, like my father, almost frail – the shells of athletes – but they are unmistakably Revie's boys.

For the first time, I'm glad my dad and I never went to Elland Road all those years ago; nothing could have beaten this. We'd earned this. We'd arrived.

After my dad died, I worried that I hadn't done enough for him in his later years. I was forever working on the television show, and I cursed myself for not having spent more time with him. When I admitted this to my mum, she said that I'd done more than I thought, more than I knew. 'And he never stopped talking about that day you went to Elland Road, you know. He loved it. He really loved it. That was special.'

'Your San Pellegrino, sir. Sir . . .?'

'Sorry. Yes.'

'The sun is in your eyes?'

'Yes. Yes, the sun. The sun.'

38

The New Season

It's mid-August. Mid-August means only one thing for foot-ball fans: the new season is approaching! I remember the excitement. The hope. Everyone level at 3 o'clock on the first Saturday; everyone starting on 0 points. Everyone happy. But this year I'm ignoring it. I'm primed with all Ronni's training. I'm ready to go for nine whole months without it. I've avoided reading about the new season, so my appetite has not been whetted. I haven't talked about it; I haven't thought about it.

But it's the first day of the season today: new kits, new players, new titles on *Match of the Day*. No! No giving in. The real hard work starts now. I'm ready. I think. But, as they say, it's going to be a marathon, not a sprint.

For a number of years in the noughties, I placed a bet on the first day of the season (it was the only bet I ever made): an accumulator – who would win each division. It made the whole season extra-special. But now football is getting easier and easier to predict. The days of Nottingham Forest or Aston Villa winning the league have gone. Everyone knows the Premier League champions in May will be one of the Big Four – Manchester United, Arsenal, Chelsea or Liverpool. And those four will be the top four, in any one of the twenty-four possible permutations.

The Premier League is almost totally predictable from top to bottom – particularly at the bottom, where everyone knows that the three promoted clubs – Stoke, West Brom and Hull this season (2008–9) – will struggle, particularly Hull. Hull's victory in the play-off final to seal their promotion to the Premier League – their first-ever season in the top flight of English football – was the last bit of football news I'd heard. I tried not to hear it, but Steven Cree, the other football fan in *Cabaret*, told me one sultry night last May, when we were in the midst of 1930s Berlin.

Since getting back from France, I've been tempted by back-page headlines in other people's newspapers on the Tube now and again but, as I've generally been cycling the eleven miles to Southwark every day, I haven't had newspapers in my face screaming about on–off transfer sagas and 'the managerial merry-go-round'. I haven't been listening to 5 Live and, after avoiding Euro 2008 and the Champions League final, I proved to myself that I could miss football and not *miss* football. I'm ready for this challenge.

To ignore the season. The whole season. The new season, the very thing I've always looked forward to. Maybe I can just do this for one season. As an experiment. A masochistic experiment. Why do I have to keep telling myself that? Because. It's. Not. Going. To. Be. Easy.

'But', I tell myself, 'it may be interesting, from a football point of view, to go the whole season without knowing a score, without looking at a league table and to see how predictable those league tables are by the end of the season.' True. 'Then you can start following the sport again – job done. Ronni happy. You've always said it's always an extra-special feeling to watch *Match of the Day* without knowing any of the scores – like some huge, delayed, multiple orgasm of football knowledge. Imagine that feeling times thirty-six!' Okay, you're on!

I guarantee Hull will go down for a start – it's scream-ingly obvious. And it's obvious that Reading will win the Championship and Leeds will win League One. Maybe I should have that bet again!

Actually, maybe I really should. Ronni didn't say anything about bets . . . But, no. If I have a bet, I'll want to know how my bet's getting on – as the old ad campaign said, 'You bet; it's more interesting.' No, no, I can't do that.

This is going to be difficult. Nine months! And then I will, officially, be a girl!

39

Horses, Clothes and Chocolate

It was becoming increasingly difficult to get hold of Alistair. I always used to know where he'd be at any given time. His life revolved around football. If I knew the football schedules, I knew Alistair's schedules. I miss his anal side, which I used to find such a help (the yin to my disorganised, artistic yang); he's now a flourishing, busy man with a rich, varied life.

It had given me time to ponder why I had such a problem with football. It was all very well getting to the root of Alistair's problem, but what was the root of mine . . .? Was it jealousy that made me dislike football so much? Maybe I thought of it as a threat. After all, football is often a man's longest-standing relationship. A wife or girlfriend or sister will always come second to football, to his beloved, blessed, wretched football club. Most young girls, no matter how much attention their father may pay them out in the garden, over a book, in the park, will see him shut off from her when the football is on. She's in the way; he can't see it. She's in the way; he can't hear it. She's in the way.

But this wasn't ever my experience. My father was away a lot – in the navy. If I'm jealous of anything, I should be jealous of ships. So is it less that and more because I didn't have a hobby that I could immerse myself in? The fact that I didn't have the pure escapism that men like Alistair get from 'The (so-called) Beautiful Game'?

I did have my ballet. That's definitely a female preserve

– or it was until *Billy Elliot* came along in his little white vest and black pumps. Some girls like horses. Childhood friends of mine rode horses every Saturday and had little china and glass figurines of horses on their bedroom window sills and drew horses in the margins of all their school books, but the national love for horses still doesn't compare with the national love for football. Girls do have other hobbies, but nothing that is so internationally loved, worshipped and obeyed.

There certainly isn't an equivalent sport for us. Or, at least, there never used to be. When I was at school, while the boys all played football, we were stuck with either hockey or netball. Hockey is another of those sports which, when we see it at the Olympic Games, makes us wonder why there isn't more airtime given to it. But it never merits the smallest of headlines in the redtops. It may as well not exist at any time outside the Games.

And netball never even gets a look-in at the Olympics. There are no famous netball players, no supposed role models being caught speeding or beating up taxi drivers.

It may be different for girls now. Today, girls are actively encouraged to play football, which I now reluctantly concede may be a good thing – it can be a fun way to expend energy, an exciting game at that level. My little girls seem to love it. But if they ever go on to show a true talent for the game, they won't be able to realise their potential in the way boys can. I realise that there are some excellent female professional footballers, but even international women's football is not given one iota of the exposure that the male game gets.

Women do seem to be more into analysing friendships: they'll talk about them over coffee, in the pub or at the water cooler – the rights and wrongs of relationships; love and Men. Men put us through agonies – like a football team. They disappoint us on a regular basis – like a football team. They thrill us occasionally – like a football team. They change their outfit once a year – like a football team. But I don't have 75,000 people watching me and my husband cooking together in the kitchen or analysing the row we had as we tried to get the children into the car for a weekend away when they just wanted to carry on watching *Peppa Pig*.

So do *I* have any sort of equivalent to football? Hmm. Well, that's a tough one. Maybe . . . chocolate. Seriously, I would happily travel all over the world trying bits of chocolate, pitting one against the other, and I could certainly eat it for ninety minutes every Wednesday night. But I wouldn't read about chocolate or listen to chocolate on the radio or watch chocolate for hours on television or watch Alan Hansen and Gary Lineker talking about chocolate week in, week out . . . So no, obviously chocolate can't be seen as my equivalent to football. The truth is, other than working and looking after my children, I don't seem to have time for anything else. There are just too many other things to do.

But rather than that lack of an equivalent being seen as a weakness, perhaps it's a positive thing. Women don't want an equivalent to football. I don't. It would take up the time of twenty other things. Football is a lifelong, full-time commitment. And that I can't understand. And never will!

40

Hull City and Plymouth Argyle

I'm managing well without football.

I've had a busy year; that helps. In the theatre; that helps. I've been poisoned, I mean helped, by Ronni; that helps.

They're Playing Our Song has kept me busy on Sundays and well away from Sky's Super Sunday football. I'd told my understudy (and Middlesbrough supporter), Eugene McCoy, about my mission – Ronni's mission – and he was interested and respectful. Initially, he didn't tell me any scores and turned over newspapers that had been left out in the theatre back page up. He even joined me in giving up the game while our run continued. Maybe Ronni *could* work her magic on the nation.

I get to late September. It's now fifty days into the new football season. Having cut down slowly since last April, I have now been totally football-free for fifty days! If I were on a chat show, people would now whoop and cheer. Friends are impressed. They help. Sometimes, people like Dan (at no. 62) and Jonny Maitland begin to ask me if I've seen a certain match and then stop themselves; they respect what I'm doing. I've been talking to taxi drivers about other things. I head them off at the pass the minute football comes up. I tell them I don't really follow it these days.

I've been talking and reading about new things. I've been playing the piano again for the first time in years. I've been playing more tennis, reading novels, reading factual books for the first time since school. I've been watching more films, inspired by Ronni's DVDs (though I still haven't seen *Trainspotting* with you-know-who). I've started cooking. I've been to lots of theatre matinees. I'm better company and spending more time in other people's company, and let's just say my top pocket is getting full of little slips of paper with numbers on them in artistic handwriting. Life, as they say in the air-conditioning world, is good.

Inevitably, after *They're Playing Our Song* comes to an end, illness strikes. It always happens after a long theatre run; suddenly the body gives in to all the coughs and colds that adrenalin has been fighting off.

I get a stinker. For several days, I stuff myself with Benylin, movies and books – Tony Harrison's poetry, Ilie Năstase's autobiography, Gyles Brandreth's Oscar Wilde detective novels. I watch hours of telly but no football. It would be so easy to slip back into it, but I stick to my guns – Ronni's guns – and I rush to turn off the football scores if they come on the *Ten O'Clock News*, scattering blankets and used tissues in my search for the ever-elusive remote. I'm doing okay. I'm doing more than okay.

Then, one night, because of the streaming nose, I can't sleep. I try everything but I just can't 'get off'. It gets to three in the morning, and I'm still just lying there. I put the radio on next to the bed. Radio 4 has gone over to the World Service – a singularly depressing and long-windedly worthy affair. I don't want music, though, and can't bear to hear a phone-in full of sleepless nutters calling in about *Star Wars* miscellanea and the price of bread in the 1970s.

So I risk a bit of Radio 5 Live. I'm woozy and weak, a little delirious from the triple whammy of the cold, the lack of sleep and the Benylin. I almost forget that they may talk about football. They're talking about theatre, as it happens. And then athletics. Getting closer . . . I'll be asleep by the time they get on to football. I am dropping off at last when I half hear the irritating 5 Live news jingle. Bits of news register with my wilting brain. And then I hear them say, 'And now the sport with Vassos . . .' I should turn it off but I'm too sleepy now to move an arm.

I'm only hearing one word in every eight anyway. I'll be asleep any second. Any second. And then I hear, '. . . and Hull City went third in the Premier League tonight after a 1–0 win over Arsenal at the Emirates stadium'.

I sit bolt upright in bed, as awake as a rabbit. Hull City third?! Beat Arsenal?! Away?! I turn my back on football for fifty days and the world turns upside down. Heaven knows what might have happened to attendances!

I can't miss this! I have to know more! I could switch on Ceefax. I sneeze copiously. No, I'll stay in bed. It'll wait till the morning. Hull City third? Maybe it's a dream . . .

When I wake in the morning, I have to know. I'm feeling a little better so I go out and get a newspaper. Ceefax won't do for this one. I need a full match report, a league table and an attendance. I know I shouldn't do it but I have to have a look and see . . . Hull City third?!

I can't even wait till I get home. On the short walk back from the little paper shop, I look at the table. It's like meeting up with an old friend. And there it is: Hull City – third!

I try to look at those higher places alone – that's all I wanted to know, after all – but my well-trained eye scans the whole table in a second. Spurs bottom with one point! This is a wonder season and I'm missing it!

I manage to stop at the Premier League. The other

tables are sitting there, full of tempting yet forbidden pleasures, like ladies in the red-light district of Amsterdam. But I can't get back into it all. Can I? Maybe just one little look . . . Ronni won't know. I look around to see that she hasn't followed me out, having somehow sensed my impending fall.

She's not there. But just the thought of her pretty little face brings me to myself. I can't let all the good work go for nothing. Fifty days – it's nothing really. Six days more than Brian Clough was manager of Leeds United . . .

This has to stop.

This has to carry on.

I put the paper in my neighbour's recycling bin (which they never take indoors) before I get back into the flat. I switch the radio back to Radio 3 and get back into bed with a Lemsip and a Sebastian Faulks.

The abstinence continues. I don't mention my little hiccup to Ronni when she calls, like my social worker, for her weekly check-up.

I do *Cinderella* at Wimbledon theatre – we do two shows a day, six days a week. There's no time to read a paper or talk to anyone about the game of football; we're too busy waving wands and turning mice into ponies. I get past Christmas without even noticing it.

And then, in February, I go into *Measure for Measure*. I'm playing the Duke, which my friend, Colin Taylor (not a football fan but nevertheless obsessed with dates and figures), tells me is the fifth biggest part in all of Shakespeare's canon. It takes some learning – again there's no time to think about football. Over breakfast, I learn lines. In bed, I learn lines. Even on the Tube with *Metros* and league tables in front of me, I learn lines. I see headlines and look away. Even at a quick glance, they do all seem the same as ever: spitting incidents, offside arguments, transfer talk – only the names change . . .

But Hull City third!! They could be top now. Or bottom, which would be a story in itself. And if . . . Stop it!

We head down to Plymouth for the final two weeks of *Measure for Measure* rehearsals before we open at the town's Theatre Royal. In the past, if I'd been somewhere like Plymouth for anything longer than two days, I'd have checked to see if there was a football match taking place. It would be nice just to go to a game and, on top of that, it would be another of the ninety-two grounds I'd visited, another name on the results, in the league tables that had become a real place in my head – a memory.

Plymouth play at Home Park – that much I know. I may never come back to Plymouth – that much I know. From the back of the local paper – I wasn't reading it, I just glanced at a headline left on a lunch table – I understand they have a home game against Reading on the Saturday . . .

I couldn't go.

Could I?

Then I hear that we'll be rehearsing on Saturday morning but we'll be free for the afternoon, the afternoon when Plymouth Argyle play Reading. What else do you do in Plymouth on a Saturday afternoon . . .? But I mustn't go, must I? I've come so far now. The Hull thing was an understandable early lapse – an accident. I wasn't well. This would be a decision . . .

No. I've promised Ronni and breaking a promise to Ronni is like breaking a mirror – you get seven years of wailing. And I'm doing so well. I'm happier without football. I really think I am. And so does she.

But one game wouldn't hurt anyone, would it? Just one little game . . .

No. There are many other things to do in Plymouth on a Saturday afternoon in March. There's shopping. And Riley's snooker hall. And at least two cinemas, and the Hoe.

But I've seen the Hoe from every angle and played so much snooker that my chin's bleeding, and there are no films out at the moment that aren't full of special effects or guns or Julie Walters. And Plymouth are playing Reading. I could . . .

No! I mustn't. I check to see what's on at the Theatre before we move in. The Welsh National Opera are there for a week. *Salome* is on again today. I've already seen it. Oh, yes! Me and opera, we're like 'that' now. I went on Wednesday night. There was Champions League football on the television in every pub in Plymouth, but I went to see a Richard Strauss opera. How about that?

It was fabulous, unforgettable and a great story, the ending of which I should have known if I had any knowledge of the Bible. But guess what? I was too busy reading about football as a kid to take in any extracurricular R.E.

Where else could I have seen a large-ish Welsh woman singing in German to the severed head of John the Baptist for fifteen minutes? Not at Home Park. Or Elland Road. Or Ninian Park, Cardiff – not to the head of John the Baptist, anyway.

But I'd seen *Salome*. I had to find something else to take my mind off the fact that I could really do with a football fix. Just one little game. Just one . . .

Before I know it, I've asked the company manager about tickets, and within hours I'm at Home Park with my fellow cast member (and QPR fan) Eliot Giuralarocca and we're sitting in the directors' box watching Plymouth Argyle play Reading. And it feels good!

I'm in comfort-blanket heaven from the first sight of the impossibly lush grass, from the first sound of the tinny tannoy, from the first time I think to myself, 'I'm in! This'll be on telly later, the result will be in the papers, on the radio, and I'm here! I'll be in the attendance – without me there would have been one less.'

I see some cameras that seem to be covering the game and don't even think about the fact that they are clearly pointing my way every so often. I'm just so happy to be here that, like a recidivist criminal going back to burglary knowing that he's probably on CCTV, it doesn't cross my mind that they may be recording me. The guilty pleasure of it all is too great.

It's a fabulous game. Pacy. Honest. Committed. It turns out (according to the chairman's charming wife) that Reading need the points to push on for a promotion place (as I'd thought!) and Plymouth need the points to pull away from the relegation dogfight. I'm tempted to look at Eliot's programme to see the league table, but I know the minute I see another league table, I'll crumble. I mustn't get hooked again. It's just one game; I can handle it.

Plymouth sneak a win thanks to a wonder goal from a player called Jamie Mackie, whom I have never heard of – a fantastic strike from thirty yards. It's one of the best goals I've ever seen. In a second, the crowd are all on their feet. For minutes afterwards the hum goes round the ground, people still marvelling at what they've seen. At the pleasure Jamie Mackie has given them.

I say to Eliot that we'll never know that feeling. As actors

– or comics – it takes time to get a response. Your performance is a series of lines or jokes that might build to a laugh or a tear. There is nothing to compare to the feeling of hitting a ball and seeing it in the back of the net a second later, bringing the crowd to their delirious feet in an instant. *That* is football.

That evening Eliot and I play snooker. We've organised a best-of-thirty-five-frames marathon for the tour. Tonight, it keeps my mind off football, off the horror of what I've done, off the shame, off the chance to go even further. I am not going back to the whole thing again. I'm not. Why should I assume that? It's just a one-off. Like meeting an ex-girlfriend for a drink. It doesn't mean we're going to start having wild sex again in hotel rooms. It was just nice to say, 'Hi! How ya doing? You look great. Nice goals!' Ronni need never know.

The next morning, I'm woken early by my landlady. She needs help with her car and thinks, just because I'm a man, that I'll be able to help. I do my best – the best anyone can do in their pyjamas when it's two degrees above freezing. But, once she's gone, I can't get back to sleep. I switch the television on; it flicks onto *The Championship*, a football-highlights programme on ITV. Ronni didn't know about this one. I didn't know about this one (it's on early in the morning) – and they're showing the Plymouth game and, within seconds, there's a shot of me in the crowd! A lingering shot of me. It's unmistakable. Unmissable. Me! Anyone watching will have seen it.

She'll know. She'll get to know. Someone will tell Ronni. What do I do? What the hell do I do? She'll go mental – seven years of wailing . . .

I do what anyone would do in the circumstances. I think, 'Oh, well, in for a penny . . .'

I watch the rest of the programme, lapping it all up, and then nip out for a paper. I buy a quality and a tabloid and devour their football sections for the rest of the day. I pore over league tables, and then various, fabulous charts full of seven months' worth of mouth-watering results, attendances, transfer gossip – it's all there. By teatime, I'm exhausted and bloated, and the newspapers lie around me, crumpled and discarded like chocolate and cake wrappers around a bulimic.

It's been an orgy of stats and nostalgia. There is no Sky TV in the flat, but if there had been I would have watched that all day too and licked the screen till I could taste football on my lips.

It turns out, by the way, that Hull are no longer third, but they are not in the bottom three, Reading are not top of the Championship, Leeds are well off the pace in League One and, as I check the standings in the World Cup qualifying groups, England are undefeated and stand proudly at the top!

It's not predictable after all. None of it. It's wonderful! And I love it!

I'm back 'on the game'.

41

Meeting on the Halfway Line

I knew that at some point I would have to tell Ronni what had happened in Plymouth. I had to tell her I was back on the soccer sauce. The *Measure for Measure* tour took me to Wolverhampton and Guildford and finally to Aberdeen. I couldn't have been much further away from Ronni in west London but, as the last show approached, I knew I couldn't put it off any longer and I knew it was going to be painful.

As soon as I got back to London, Ronni rang wanting to know how I was getting on.

'Why don't we meet up,' I said. 'It's been ages since I saw you.'

'That'd be lovely. Do you want to come over to the house?'

'No. Why don't we go and eat somewhere?'

'Oh, that would be really nice!'

'How about La Maison de Juliette again?'

'No, I'd rather not . . .'

'But it's really nice, Ronni. And very handy.'

'I . . . I can't go back there.'

'Why not?'

'I don't think the waiter likes me very much.'

'Oh . . .?'

'He told me I was fussy and I . . . Oh, well, never mind. How about H2O?'

'Great. Tomorrow?'

'Perfect.'

I had suggested that we meet in public as there would be less chance she would go nuts when she heard my confession. So now I'm sitting in the trendy glass and chrome of H2O, waiting for her to come back from the toilet. It's a busy lunchtime. We've had small talk and baby talk but as yet there's been no mention of football. And no sign of our food. I toy with the idea of not telling her about Plymouth, of just pretending I'm still on the football wagon. But my conscience gets the better of me. I resolve to tell her as soon as she gets back from the toilet. As soon as she gets back. As soon as . . . Unless she doesn't ask me. Then I could pretend it never . . .

'That's better. So, how are you coping without the old you-know-what?' she asks me.

I look at her from under my eyebrows.

'How long has it been now, Ali? Nearly a year? How many days exactly?'

'323,' I guess.

'That's brilliant, Ali! You've done so well!'

'Ronni? Do you remember how I told you that a friend of mine once said to me that to get what you want from someone you have to stroke the cat before you hit it?'

'Metaphorically, yes.'

'Well, she was a Christian, this girl, and . . .'

'Oh, God!'

'Don't! Listen!'

'I'm listening.'

'Well, she also told me that if you could understand why someone was the way they were, then you could accept their foibles.'

Ronni's gone very quiet. Either she knows what's

coming or she is thinking about something else. It's always hard to tell with her.

'If you know someone was never taught manners,' I say, 'it's easier to accept that they're bad-mannered; if you know that someone was kicked on the leg by a horse when they were five, you understand why they're scared of horses; if you know someone was born in Stoke-on-Trent, you understand why they might have a chip on their shoulder.'

'Why are you telling me all this?'

'I went to a game.'

'What game?'

'A football game. A match. In Plymouth. Plymouth v. Reading.'

'WHAT!!!'

'And it was great!'

'YOU WENT TO A GAME?'

'Yes. Plymouth v. Reading. Plymouth won 2–1 . . .'

'Never mind the score!'

'I'm sorry!'

'But, Ali, you were doing so well . . .'

'I know!'

'Ochh! I can't believe you went to a game.'

I look her in the eyes, giving nothing away.

'After all our hard work!'

'I know. I just . . .'

'Well, one game, I suppose that's okay. As long as you didn't go back to football full-time because of it.'

I look her in the eyes again.

'I kind of did.'

'I don't believe this!'

'It had been almost a year and I just cracked and . . .'

'You promised!'

'I know, Ronni. And I tried really hard and you're right: football doesn't really make sense. I've seen that and I'm willing to cut down on my football, but I can't give it up. It's too ingrained.'

'It's just habit!'

'It is a habit; it is an addiction. But I can't give it up, Ronni. I can't.'

'Because you're weak; you're all weak! Men! Och, smokers say this, drug addicts and alcoholics say this at some point – "Ooh, it's too hard! I can't give it up." But thousands of them, millions of them see it through! And they and their partners and their families and their work colleagues breathe a huge, fresh sigh of relief.'

'Ronni, we're all addicted to something.'

'I'm not.'

'Maybe you are and you don't know it.'

'There's nothing I couldn't live without!'

'Chocolate?'

'Apart from chocolate.'

'As addictions go, football isn't so bad, Ronni. I mean, would you rather be with a heroin addict or a football addict?'

'It's a close one.'

'Seriously!'

'Seriously!'

Our waitress comes over to us and says, 'I'm sorry about the delay with your food,' with a look that unmistakably also says, 'I forgot to put the order on the order board.'

We smile back a 'That's fine', keen to be left alone.

'I'm sorry, Ronni.'

'I can't believe you went to a match. When was this?'

'When we were in Plymouth.'

'Yes, but when was that?'

'Four weeks ago.'

'And you enjoyed it?'

'Yes.'

'It felt good, did it?'

'It felt good, Ronni. Yes, it did.'

'And did you think of me at all while you were doing this?'

'Of course.'

'What it might do to me? To "us"? What it meant?'

'Yes.'

'No. No, you didn't, did you?'

'I did! I really did!! I agonised!'

'After all we've been through together.'

'I know.'

'But you just couldn't resist, could you?'

'It was just sort of there. In front of me. On a plate. I didn't feel I could say no.'

'Of course you could have said no! You're a grown man, with your own decision-making powers. You can do what you want!'

'What *you* want,' I mumble.

'What?'

'Nothing.'

'I suppose somebody forced you into it.'

'No, it was my own choice.'

'Oh, God!'

'I was miles from home and the ground was just there and I tried to resist it but something just got the better of me. I'm so sorry. I didn't want to hurt you; that's the last thing I wanted, you know that.'

'Four weeks ago?'

'About that, yes.'

'And you didn't tell me till now?'

'No, I thought . . . I thought . . .'

'Thought you'd get away with it?

'Yes. No! But, Ronni, football doesn't really harm any-one.'

'It stunts your growth.'

'That's smoking!'

'No! Listen to me, Ali. It stunts your emotional growth, your intellectual growth. It's safe and warm and cosy, and it reminds you of when you were a kid and all that, but think of the hours you've wasted over the years, Ali. So many things you could have done and read about and seen – but no, you wanted to be able to say to strangers in the pub that Rochdale United were in with a chance of making the play-offs in the Premier League.'

'It's League Two.'

'Whatever it is!'

'And it's just Rochdale not Rochdale United.'

'What does it matter?!'

'It matters to me! And to everyone in Rochdale. And to anyone who likes football. Okay, you've made me see that football isn't always a grown-up thing. I agree that it's been overhyped and there's too much of it on television and the players are overpaid and bad role models and all that – and I can now take it or leave it. For which I thank you, Ronni. And I've done things this year I would never have done. And I've seen things I wouldn't have otherwise seen – including a man balancing on another man's head on one hand in a pair of Union Jack pants.'

'What?'

243

'*La Clique*; you've got to see it. But the thing is . . .'

Our waitress is suddenly at our side again. 'Would you like any more drinks?'

'No, we're fine . . .' says Ronni, just sharply enough to let the waitress know she should leave us alone unless she has food in her hands.

'. . . the thing is, Ronni, I need football.'

'You don't!'

'Men need it.'

'Listen to me! You don't need it! Ali, you don't need it! You were richer without it; you said so!'

'And it's actually the most exposed sport because it is probably the best sport. And that's why they can never make a good film about it, because it's better drama than drama . . .'

'Listen to me, Ali! Are you listening?'

'Yes.'

'Football isn't drama; it's commercialism and marketing – cynical marketing. It exploits kids and parents and forces them to buy a new shirt every month for their kid.'

'That was stopped.'

'By who?'

'I don't know, Tony Blair or Gok Wan or someone. But listen, Ronni . . .'

'No, you listen, Ali.'

'No, you listen!'

'Ali, people are looking.'

'Shhh then.'

'Don't "shush" me!'

'Listen, Ronni! Ultimately men need football and women need men to need football. Mitchell and Webb were wrong.'

'What have Mitchell and Webb got to do with anything?'

'They did this sketch about football . . .'

'Oh, yes. I've seen it. It's brilliant!'

'It is brilliant but it's flawed.'

'Why?'

'Because they say it's a bad thing that football never ends, but it's actually a good thing that football never ends. It's eternal. That's why it gives men hope. That's why we love it. It doesn't die. I will cut down. Like I say, I'll always be grateful to you for that – but it is a part of me and without it, without it entirely, I'm someone else. Aren't I?'

There was a pause. Ronni looked at me like she understood.

'I did nearly twelve months. When we were together, I couldn't have done twelve days.'

'Twelve hours.'

'Twelve seconds.'

'Twelve milliseconds.'

'Twelve nanoseconds.'

And suddenly she was smiling. My lovely, beautiful old friend was smiling again.

'I was starting to miss you.'

'Being on tour for so long?'

'No. Not being you. I mean, you were you. But I'm glad the old you is back.'

'Well, yes. But I don't think I'll be quite as obsessed as before.'

'Well, that's . . . perfect.'

'And I'll always have my memories. I'll always have that seven-year-old in me, playing with my dad under the cherry blossom and dreaming of Leeds. That'll never go away, will it?'

'No, of course not. And d'you know what?'

'Oh, my God!'

'What is it, Ali?'

I paused and stared at the just-opened door.

'It can't be.'

'Ali, what is it?'

'That guy looks just like . . . no, what would he be doing here?'

'Who? God, you're annoying sometimes, Ali!'

'That guy in the long black coat . . .'

'Yes . . .?'

'He looks just like Peter Lorimer!'

'Peter who?'

42

The Final Whistle

So, the results of my experiment with Ali? Well, I can't say he's totally cured of his addiction – and I'm glad of that now – but I do think he has come to realise that, if abused, football destroys lives.

And I've realised that it is not necessarily good for the health of a wife or girlfriend if the men in their lives have no access to football at all. God knows men can be grumpy enough with it. What would they be like without it?

Even if the impossible happened and football became illegal, it would simply go underground. It would be like the Prohibition era in the US. There would be police raids on smoky basements where unshaven men would sit around poker tables swapping football cards and watching foreign matches on illicit TV channels. Suffice to say, it would all become even more important and precious than it is now – if that's possible.

But, please, can we non-football lovers at least be listened to? The complete and utter overkill of what is essentially a decent and exciting game is in danger of driving us mad!

Failing that, our only hope is to somehow make the game more interesting. I give you some of my suggestions . . .

RONNI'S TEN WAYS TO MAKE FOOTBALL MORE INTERESTING

(1) Every time a player gets a yellow card, he has to do a party piece in front of the whole crowd: sing a little song, do a dance, recite a poem or perform a magic trick.

(2) Every time a player is given a red card he has to show his bottom.

(3) Every time a player is booked for dissent, his team's goalposts are widened by six feet. If he protests, they are widened by another five feet.

(4) If a player is sent off for dissent, his team's goalkeeper has to have one hand tied behind his back or his feet tied together.

(5) If there are no goals after twenty minutes, one player from each team must leave and return dressed in full ballet regalia – complete with tutu.

(6) If there are no goals by half-time, the angry, gum-chewing managers have to come on and play in their suits, but wearing novelty animal slippers as footwear.

(7) If there are no goals at full-time, then each team has to buy their fans in the crowd a drink.

(8) In all friendly matches, each player has to be joined by their leg to the player playing in the same position in the opposing team, so everyone is playing a three-legged match and, in essence, has to tackle themselves. (Well, friendliness is all about togetherness . . .)

(9) Internationals should be played on thick, bouncy foam pitches, and players must wear glittery shorts.

(10) Games being shown on TV must have commentary from Joanna Lumley or John Hurt. Anyone who sounds like John Motson (or actually is John Motson) must be banned immediately.

And if the man in your life thinks that some of the suggestions on that list are actually good ideas, he is probably now taking football a little less seriously and, hopefully, his addiction is under control. He's no longer in thrall to the game or to his past. And now, for improving his life, you are the best girlfriend he's ever had – better even than football.

Acknowledgements

For getting this book from their heads to the page, Ronni and Alistair would like to thank Charlie Page and Smokey, Marion McGowan, Kay McGowan, Jonathan Maitland, Gerard Hall, Alan Francis, Jonny Geller and Hannah Griffiths, Jane and Derek Ancona.

Alistair would also like to thank:

Harvey, Reaney, Madeley, Bremner, Charlton, Hunter, Lorimer, Clarke, Jones, Giles, Gray, E.
Subs:Yorath, Bates, McQueen, Sprake, Cooper, Cherry, Gray, F.